GOD WITHOUT RELIGION

Toward a better understanding of God

Marie C. A. M. PIERRE

Unless otherwise noted, all biblical texts used in this work are taken from the King James Version (KJV).

ISBN Kindle Version: 978-1-7381632-9-8

ISBN Paperback version: 978-1-7381632-8-1

Published by: Celestial Guide Publications

This book or part of the book, except the biblical texts, may not be reproduced or used in any way without mentioning the name of the author.

TABLE OF CONTENTS

Greetings 5

CHAPTER I - God Is the Creator 9

CHAPTER II - God Created the Earth 15

CHAPTER III - God Gives Us Grace 22

CHAPTER IV - God Is Love 26

CHAPTER V - God Created Us for Domination 30

CHAPTER VI - God Is Faithful 35

CHAPTER VII - God Is Omnipotent, Omniscient, and Omnipresent 40

CHAPTER VIII - God Just Asks Us to Believe in Him and in His Son, Jesus 45

CHAPTER IX - God Does Not Accuse Us 52

CHAPTER X - God Wants Us to Be His People and Live in Unity 57

CHAPTER XI - God Wants Us to Dominate in All Things 65

CHAPTER XII - God Wants Us to Resolve Our Conflicts and in Love 70

CHAPTER XIII - God Wants Us to Be Free 77

CHAPTER XIV - God Gives Us Life, Health, and Light 84

CHAPTER XV - God Lives in Us 93

CHAPTER XVI - God Gives Us His Love, His Joy, His Peace 100

CHAPTER XVII - God Gives Us Wisdom, Knowledge, and Understanding 108

CHAPTER XVIII - God Gives Us Boldness, Love, and Wisdom 115

CHAPTER XIX - God Offers Us a Life of Abundance 120

CHAPTER XX - God Commands Us to Glorify Him Always 126

CHAPTER XXI - God Puts His Spirit in Us 131

CHAPTER XXII - Sons and Daughters of God by Adoption 137

CHAPTER XXIII - God is Sovereign – Let Us Glorify Him!.. 143

CHAPTER XXIV - God Wants Us to Be Good and Kind...... 151

CHAPTER XXV - He is The God of The Impossible 157

Final Words 164

Key Biblical Verses 168

Author's Note 170

GREETINGS

Dear readers,

For some time now, I have been hearing and reading comments, discussions, and opinions from many people about religion and faith in God that left me concerned.

I believe that criticism can help change things in a context where we are looking for change, a solution to a problem. I also understand that critics can build, as well as destroy, even the little that already exists, if the shot is not well framed. Through these writings, I want to bring you this good news:

« **God is not religion.** »

Were you aware of this? I repeat:

« **God is not religion** »

I am aware that religion was supposed to be God's ambassador to the world, the channel through which God's message is received. But again, this would not have changed the fact that:

« God is not religion. »

I have not given myself the mission to talk to you about religion or to tell you that it has failed or that it has succeeded, that man has manipulated it or not, that it has been instrumentalized or not. No way. Through this book, I gave myself the mission to address what God is, and what he wants for us, according to his Word written in the Bible.

As a believer and member of a Christian church, I have dedicated myself to knowing God, to doing his will, and to becoming who he has called me to be. I know that Scripture is the key to this success, and I thank God for doing me so much good on this path. Every day, I read my Bible and experience pleasant moments in His kingdom. God has so many extraordinary things in store for us, but instead of enjoying them, we focus on reacting to hearsay, yet I ask the Lord to still grant us the chance to soak up his grace. This is an invitation to turn our backs on various distractions and put our focus on what really matters about God.

God is his Word.

God wants us to have a perfect relationship with him.

God wants us to be gods, to have dominion over all things.

God wants us to accept his grace, which will allow our reconciliation with Him.

God wants us to accept this renewal that He is preparing to do in us through His Holy Spirit.

God wants us to be filled with wisdom, intelligence, and knowledge.

God wants us to manifest His power on earth.

God wants us to live in peace, joy, and abundance.

God wants us to be successful in everything we do.

God wants us to live in unity.

God wants us to be saved.

So, let's conquer all these things, and more, by reading through these writings.

The world is currently facing its own downfall. However, God offers us the solution. Knowing God without the disputes of religions is an effective way to grasp this solution and to understand the functioning and expectations of God related to ourselves.

Interreligious disputes drive us away from God and, in some cases, even push us away from God. In the meantime, one thing is certain: God's love for humanity does not change.

When I wake up in the morning and contemplate the nature and complexity of the human being, I think it is impossible not to have a great, supreme, very wise, mysterious God behind these wonders. However, few people believe in Him because He is often confused with religion.

Let's do it differently, with **God without religion**.

Let's go! I wish you a good reading.

If you have any questions about these writings, contact us at mdimpact.community@gmail.com and I will have the great pleasure of deepening this knowledge with you.

May the fullness of God's grace in Jesus Christ be upon you!

CHAPTER I
GOD IS THE CREATOR

You have probably already heard, like me, that the universe was created by cellular multiplication or following a famous explosion (the Big Bang theory). My husband told me one day (and I agree with him), "I have never seen or heard of a collision between two random objects producing something else beautiful, structured, and organized, like a collision between two old, ugly vehicles producing a brand new Lamborghini or Rolls Royce." Some parents refer to their children as "unwanted children" because they did not choose to have them for various reasons. They then speak of children conceived by "accident." In this case, I would say that these "accidents" have integrated the order and discipline of creation, which is why they produce these extraordinary beings (these children). In this same vein, I am thinking of grains that have unintentionally fallen into fertile soil and which, by happy coincidence, are covered and have access to the nutrients they need. Descartes would say, "The same causes always produce the same effects under the same conditions."

In my opinion, it is everyone's responsibility to decide which theory to believe. But this extraordinary, incomprehensible, marvelous, ordered universe cannot be the result of chance. I believe a supreme being planned this.

I read on Wikipedia that the solar system was formed a little less than 4.6 billion years ago from the collapse of a molecular cloud, followed by the formation of a protoplanetary disk, according to the nebula hypothesis.

I respect the efforts made by our researchers because it is God himself who gave us the freedom to choose, and despite our distance from his plan of life, he leaves us this freedom. One should not be more royalist than the King himself, they say. However, here I present to you some facts on which my faith is based:

- I have never seen or heard of a person who was not born from the union of a man and a woman. Have you?

- I think about the complexity of my heart, my lungs, and my kidneys. Do you know that our heart is like a pump that works 7 days a week, 24 hours a day, for the entire duration of our life on earth without fuel supply or specific maintenance? I have a lot of respect for those who suffer from any insufficiency or failure in their body. My father died at age 79 of heart failure. I am dealing here with the general (although solutions are offered by God in these specific cases; we will talk about them a little later).

- Have you thought about how plants work, about the complexity of the air-plant-soil relationship? Plants consume the carbon dioxide exhaled by humans to produce the oxygen that humans need for respiration.

- Have you ever thought about the organization of the different parts of your body? The place of your eyes, for example? If you were the Creator, where would you have placed them? As Dr. Mike Murdock likes to say, imagine how we would function if our eyes were placed under our feet. I'll leave it up to you to think about it.

So many questions and more push me to believe that there is a wise man, a supreme, perfect, and unique being at the origin of all these wonders. And for me, it is God.

Indeed, the biblical story tells how God created everything and defined the beginning of all things. Let's read these portions of the Bible.

BIBLICAL REFERENCES

Genesis 1: 1-31, 2: 1-3

In the beginning God created the heaven and the earth. And the earth was without form, and void; and darkness was upon the face of the deep. And the Spirit of God moved upon the face of the waters.

And God said, Let there be light: and there was light. And God saw the light, that it was good: and God divided the light from the darkness. And God called the light Day, and the darkness he called Night. **And the evening and the morning were the first day.**

And God said, Let there be a firmament in the midst of the waters, and let it divide the waters from the waters. And God made the firmament, and divided the waters which were under the firmament from the waters which were above the firmament: and it was so. And God called the firmament Heaven. **And the evening and the morning were the second day.**

And God said, let the waters under the heaven be gathered together unto one place, and let the dry land appear: and it was so. And God called the dry land Earth; and the gathering together of the waters called he Seas: and God saw that it was good. And God said, Let the earth bring forth grass, the herb yielding seed, and the fruit tree yielding fruit after his kind, whose seed is in itself, upon the earth: and it was so. And the earth brought forth grass, and herb yielding seed after his kind, and the tree yielding fruit, whose seed was in itself, after his kind: and God saw that it was good. **And the evening and the morning were the third day.**

And God said, Let there be lights in the firmament of the heaven to divide the day from the night; and let them be for signs, and for seasons, and for days, and years: And let them be for lights in the firmament of the heaven to give light upon the earth: and it was so. And God made two great lights; the greater light to rule the day, and the lesser light to rule the night: he made the stars also. And God set them in the firmament of the heaven to give light upon the earth, And to rule over the day and over the night, and to divide the light from the darkness: and God saw that it was good. **And the evening and the morning were the fourth day.**

And God said, Let the waters bring forth abundantly the moving creature that hath life, and fowl that may fly above the earth in the open firmament of heaven. And God created great whales, and every living creature that moveth, which the waters brought forth abundantly, after their kind, and every winged fowl after his kind: and God saw that it was good. And God blessed them, saying, Be fruitful, and multiply, and fill the waters in the seas, and let fowl multiply in the earth. **And the evening and the morning were the fifth day.**

And God said, Let the earth bring forth the living creature after his kind, cattle, and creeping thing, and beast of the earth after his kind: and it was so. And God made the beast of the earth after his kind, and cattle after their kind, and every thing that creepeth upon the earth after his kind: and God saw that it was good. And God said, Let us make man in our image, after our likeness: and let them have dominion over the fish of the sea, and over the fowl of the air, and over the cattle, and over all the earth, and over every creeping thing that creepeth upon the earth. So God created man in his own image, in the image of God created he him; male and female created he them. And God blessed them, and God said unto them, Be fruitful, and multiply, and replenish the earth, and subdue it: and have dominion over the fish of the sea, and over the fowl of the air, and over every living thing that moveth upon the earth. And God said, Behold, I have given you every herb bearing seed, which is upon the face of all the earth, and every tree, in the which is the fruit of a tree yielding seed; to you it shall be for meat. And to every beast of the earth, and to every fowl of the air, and to every thing that creepeth upon the earth, wherein there is life, I have given every green herb for meat: and it was so. And God saw every thing that he had made, and, behold, it was very good. **And the evening and the morning were the sixth day.**

Thus the heavens and the earth were finished, and all the host of them. And on the seventh day God ended his work which he had made; and he rested on the seventh day from all his work which he had made. And God blessed the seventh day, and sanctified it: because that in it he had rested from all his work which God created and made.

CHAPTER II
GOD CREATED THE EARTH

Every time I have the privilege of reading an extract from the Bible talking about creation or scientific reports presenting the way the earth works, my being is amazed at the wisdom, mystery, and perfection hidden behind all these beautiful works. However, if reading these elements amazes you, then look at creation or even an element of creation and try to understand how it works. Wow! It's extraordinary. The beauty spectacle that nature offers us in autumn (in Quebec, for example) is a perfect example. Science is doing a fabulous job of bringing creation back to human understanding and studying possible reaction equations (as children, we learn to cook by making mixtures here and there, even if we are unable to consume what comes out). I invite you to take a walk in place: read about the functioning of your heart, your lungs, or your kidneys—just one small element of creation—and then take a moment to describe the finesse of wisdom, of power, and of the love hidden there.

Let's take the heart because my father died from a cardiovascular shock during a surgical procedure. I really like this organ, as it is precious for life. It has to pump the blood constantly without stopping for us to continue the ride of life.

Read on the blog "La vie naturelle" on October 3, 2023

The heart acts like a pump; it propels blood throughout the body, which will follow a very specific path. For this, the heart has a real "electrical circuit," starting from the sinus node located in the upper left corner of the right atrium to the atrioventricular node, which is located between the atriums and the ventricles. The electric current then travels through two distinct beams, allowing the contraction of the ventricles.

Oxygenated blood arrives at the heart via the four pulmonary veins loaded with oxygenated blood poor in carbon dioxide and begins its circuit in the left atrium. It then passes into the left ventricle via the mitral valve and then, through ventricular muscle contraction, ejects blood to the aorta, which is a large vessel originating from the left ventricle and forming the aortic arch above the heart. The aorta artery then gives rise to the different arteries and blood capillaries, which carry the blood to the tissues and organs where gas exchanges and the passage of nutrients to the cells take place.

The blood, thus relieved of its oxygen and loaded with carbon dioxide, rises towards the heart through the veins, which join to form the inferior vena cava and the superior vena cava. This blood passes through the atrium, then the right ventricle, and exits the heart towards the lungs via the pulmonary arteries to allow the expiration of CO_2 and the recovery of oxygen. The cycle can then resume.

This is fabulous, my friends!

Just the heart! I leave it to you to seek out other information on the functioning of your being. I'm not a chef, but I know that good dishes are made with a lot of love.

The icing on the cake is that God created us in his image according to his likeness and decided that we have the wisdom, intelligence, and knowledge to function on earth with this same divine dimension. God created us to be gods. This is why he rested on the seventh day (after the creation of man). He is only waiting for us to manifest this divinity, and nature awaits this manifestation with ardent desire (Romans 8:19–21).

BIBLICAL REFERENCES

Jeremiah 10: 12-13

He hath made the earth by his power, he hath established the world by his wisdom, and hath stretched out the heavens by his discretion. When he uttereth his voice, there is a multitude of waters in the heavens, and he causeth the vapours to ascend from the ends of the earth; he maketh lightnings with rain, and bringeth forth the wind out of his treasures.

Romans 11:33-36

O the depth of the riches both of the wisdom and knowledge of God! How unsearchable are his judgments, and his ways past finding out! *For who hath known the mind of the Lord? Or who hath been his counsellor?* Or who hath first given to him, and it shall be recompensed unto him again? For of him, and through him, and to him, are all things: to whom be glory forever. Amen.

Jeremiah 51:15-16

He hath made the earth by his power, he hath established the world by his wisdom, and hath stretched out the heaven by his understanding. When he uttereth his voice, there is a multitude of waters in the heavens; and he causeth the vapours to ascend from the ends of the earth: he maketh lightnings with rain, and bringeth forth the wind out of his treasures.

Isaiah 40:28-29

Hast thou not known? Hast thou not heard, that the everlasting God, the LORD, the Creator of the ends of the earth, fainteth not, neither is weary? There is no searching of his understanding. He giveth power to the faint; and to them that have no might he increaseth strength.

Jeremiah 32:17-19

Ah Lord GOD! behold, thou hast made the heaven and the earth by thy great power and stretched out arm, and there is nothing too hard for thee: Thou shewest loving kindness unto thousands, and recompensest the iniquity of the fathers into the bosom of their children after them: the Great, the Mighty God, the LORD of hosts, is his name, Great in counsel, and mighty in work: for thine eyes are open upon all the ways of the sons of men: to give every one according to his ways, and according to the fruit of his doings:

Proverbs 8:12-31

I wisdom dwell with prudence, and find out knowledge of witty inventions. The fear of the LORD is to hate evil: pride, and arrogancy, and the evil way, and the froward mouth, do I hate. Counsel is mine, and sound wisdom: I am understanding; I have strength. By me kings reign, and princes decree justice. By me princes rule, and nobles, even all the judges of the earth. **I love them that love me; and those that seek me early shall find me**. Riches and honour are with me; yea, durable riches and righteousness. My fruit is better than gold, yea, than fine gold; and my revenue than choice silver. I lead in the way of righteousness, in the midst of the paths of judgment: That I may cause those that love me to inherit substance; and I will fill their treasures. The LORD possessed me in the beginning of his way, before his works of old. I was set up from everlasting, from the beginning, or ever the earth was. When there were no depths, I was brought forth; when there were no fountains abounding with water. Before the mountains were settled, before the hills was I brought forth: While as yet he had not made the earth, nor the fields, nor the highest part of the dust of the world. When he prepared the heavens, I was there: when he set a compass upon the face of the depth: When he established the clouds above: when he strengthened the fountains of the deep: When he gave to the sea his decree, that the waters should not pass his commandment: when he appointed the foundations of the earth: Then I was by him, as one brought up with him: and I was daily his delight, rejoicing always before him; Rejoicing in the habitable part of his earth; and my delights were with the sons of men.

Romans 8: 19-23

For **the earnest expectation of the creature waiteth for the manifestation of the sons of God**. For the creature was made subject to vanity, not willingly, but by reason of him who hath subjected the same in hope, Because the creature itself also shall be delivered from the bondage of corruption into the glorious liberty of the children of God. For we know that the whole creation groaneth and travaileth in pain together until now. And not only they, but ourselves also, which have the firstfruits of the Spirit, even we ourselves groan within ourselves, waiting for the adoption, to wit, the redemption of our body.

CHAPTER III
GOD GIVES US GRACE

God's grace in our lives is a wonderful gift meant to reconcile us with our Creator. However, there is a little important thing in this reconciliation: we were divine creatures before our separation from God, but in grace, we are called to be sons and daughters and, therefore, heirs of the kingdom of God. It's extraordinary. Indeed, grace is offered in Christ Jesus (Ephesians 2:4–9) to those who receive and accept Christ as their savior and king. In this grace, God sends us a wave superior to that which he sends to his creatures. He calls us to be his sons and daughters, born by the grace we receive in Christ. This grace is complete, and it completes everything in us. It covers everything that could cause us guilt, fear, weakness, sadness, poverty, anxiety, hatred, doubt, suffering, and much more. We are called today to be aware of it and to take full advantage of it. Remember that those who are in Christ are covered by a filter in the eyes of God so that when God looks at us, he sees Christ obedient to the point of death on the Cross for our sanctification. There is just one key to open this door of grace, to enter and remain there eternally: Accept grace.

BIBLICAL REFERENCES

Ephesians 2: 4-10

But God, who is rich in mercy, for his great love wherewith he loved us, Even when we were dead in sins, hath quickened us together with Christ, (by grace ye are saved;) And hath raised us up together, and made us sit together in heavenly places in Christ Jesus: That in the ages to come he might shew the exceeding riches of his grace in his kindness toward us through Christ Jesus. For by grace are ye saved through faith; and that not of yourselves: it is the gift of God: Not of works, lest any man should boast. For we are his workmanship, created in Christ Jesus unto good works, which God hath before ordained that we should walk in them.

John 1: 11-13

He came unto his own, and his own received him not. But as many as received him, to them gave he power to become the sons of God, even to them that believe on his name: Which were born, not of blood, nor of the will of the flesh, nor of the will of man, but of God.

Romans 5: 1-11

Therefore being justified by faith, we have peace with God through our Lord Jesus Christ: By whom also we have access by faith into this grace wherein we stand, and rejoice in hope of the glory of God. And not only so, but we glory in tribulations also: knowing that tribulation worketh patience; And patience, experience; and experience, hope: And hope maketh not ashamed; because the love of God is shed abroad in our hearts by the Holy Ghost which is given unto us. For when we were yet without strength, in due time Christ died for the ungodly. For scarcely for a righteous man will one die: yet peradventure for a good man some would even dare to die. But God commendeth his love toward us, in that, while we were yet sinners, Christ died for us. Much more then, being now justified by his blood, we shall be saved from wrath through him. For if, when we were enemies, we were reconciled to God by the death of his Son, much more, being reconciled, we shall be saved by his life. And not only so, but we also joy in God through our Lord Jesus Christ, by whom we have now received the atonement.

Romans 8: 14-17

For as many as are led by the Spirit of God, they are the sons of God. For ye have not received the spirit of bondage again to fear; but ye have received the Spirit of adoption, whereby we cry, Abba, Father. The Spirit itself beareth witness with our spirit, that we are the children of God: And if children, then heirs; heirs of God, and joint-heirs with Christ; if so be that we suffer with him, that we may be also glorified together.

John 3: 17-19

For God sent not his Son into the world to condemn the world; but that the world through him might be saved. He that believeth on him is not condemned: but he that believeth not is condemned already, because he hath not believed in the name of the only begotten Son of God. And this is the condemnation, that light is come into the world, and men loved darkness rather than light, because their deeds were evil.

CHAPTER IV

GOD IS LOVE

Have you ever thought about the fact that, somewhere, there is a "someone" who loves you beyond measure? Who is ready to do anything for you to live comfortably?

Yes, he does exist; he is there, and it is God. And he truly loves you with a love that goes beyond imaginable limits. There is nothing you can hope for from a person who loves you that is not contained in their love for you, and this is in a dimension higher than your imagination.

- The sacrifice of His only son is perfect proof of His love for all of us.

- The disposition of His being (the Holy Spirit) within us is a sign of love for us that passes understanding.

- Forgiveness of all our sins.

- The constant and eternal surveillance that he offers us by making Himself our shepherd and our perfect protector.

- The arrangement of angels around us.

- The particularity of our creation.

- Our God of truth tells us that he gives us everything in Jesus Christ. It is important to draw your attention to some particularities concerning his love:

    - He places His Spirit in us with the mission of producing in us, among other things, His love; then He tells us perfect love banishes fear and does not suspect evil; He tells us again, love brings joy, peace, patience, faith, kindness, benevolence, temperance...

    - He also tells us to be filled with the Spirit by speaking to us in psalms, hymns, and spiritual songs and by singing and celebrating the praises of the Lord.

    - He also tells us, "Come to me with your burden, and I will give you well-deserved rest." Who you are at this moment does not matter to Him because He wants to take responsibility for who you should be according to His plan of hope and peace that He has designed, in particular, for your life. Come and see for yourselves.

BIBLICAL REFERENCES

1 John 4: 7-10

Beloved, let us love one another: for love is of God; and every one that loveth is born of God, and knoweth God. He that loveth not knoweth not God; for God is love. In this was manifested the love of God toward us, because that God sent his only begotten Son into the world, that we might live through him. Herein is love, not that we loved God, but that he loved us, and sent his Son to be the propitiation for our sins.

John 3: 16

For God so loved the world, that he gave his only begotten Son, that whosoever believeth in him should not perish, but have everlasting life.

Galatians 5: 22-23

But the fruit of the Spirit is love, joy, peace, longsuffering, gentleness, goodness, faith, Meekness, temperance: against such there is no law.

1 Corinthians 13: 4-8

Charity (Love) suffereth long, and is kind; charity envieth not; charity (Love) vaunteth not itself, is not puffed up, Doth not behave itself unseemly, seeketh not her own, is not easily provoked, **thinketh no evil**; Rejoiceth not in iniquity, but rejoiceth in the truth; Beareth all things, believeth all things, hopeth all things, endureth all things. Charity (Love) never faileth:

but whether there be prophecies, they shall fail; whether there be tongues, they shall cease; whether there be knowledge, it shall vanish away.

Romans 5: 6-8

For when we were yet without strength, in due time Christ died for the ungodly. For scarcely for a righteous man will one die: yet peradventure for a good man some would even dare to die. But God commendeth his love toward us, in that, while we were yet sinners, Christ died for us.

Matthew 11: 28-30

Come unto me, all ye that labour and are heavy laden, and I will give you rest. Take my yoke upon you, and learn of me; for I am meek and lowly in heart: and ye shall find rest unto your souls. For my yoke is easy, and my burden is light.

CHAPTER V

GOD CREATED US FOR DOMINATION

Be fruitful, multiply, fill the earth, and subdue and dominate it constitutes the first command that man received from God after his creation. But at some point in our functioning, man subjected the earth to another domination by disobeying the ordinances of God. However, God's faithfulness is eternal. He doesn't take back what he gave. So in Christ Jesus, our King and Lord, He gives us back His Spirit, a spirit of adoption, so that we now function as His own sons and daughters. The presence of His Spirit in us gives us the status of sons today. Nature is just waiting for us to restore it.

God knows that we were sinners and that we lived without heeding His ordinances. He sent Jesus, who offered himself on the cross, to be the filter through which God looks at us and through which He sees us as holy. This privilege is granted to those who accept Christ as their Lord, according to what is written in John 1 verses 12–13: "to those who received him, to those who believe in his name, he gave power to become children of God born of the will of God."

Your place is in Christ, and your ability to rule according to God's plan of redemption is in Christ. God's plan of redemption is for you too.

BIBLICAL REFERENCES

Genesis 1: 27-28

So God created man in his own image, in the image of God created he him; male and female created he them. And God blessed them, and God said unto them, Be fruitful, and multiply, and replenish the earth, and **subdue it:** and **have dominion over** the fish of the sea, and over the fowl of the air, and over every living thing that moveth upon the earth.

Genesis 6: 3

And the LORD said, My spirit shall not always strive with man, for that he also is flesh: yet his days shall be an hundred and twenty years.

Acts 1: 4-5

And, being assembled together with them, commanded them that they should not depart from Jerusalem, but wait for the promise of the Father, which, saith he, ye have heard of me. For John truly baptized with water; but **ye shall be baptized with the Holy Ghost not many days hence**.

Romans 8: 14

For as many as are led by the Spirit of God, they are the sons of God.

Romans 8: 19-21

For the earnest expectation of the creature waiteth for the manifestation of the sons of God. For the creature was made subject to vanity, not willingly, but by reason of him who hath subjected the same in hope, Because the creature itself also shall be delivered from the bondage of corruption into the glorious liberty of the children of God.

Ecclesiastes 10: 5-7

There is an evil which I have seen under the sun, as an error which proceedeth from the ruler: Folly is set in great dignity, and the rich sit in low place. I have seen servants upon horses, and **princes walking as servants** upon the earth.

Psalms 82: 6-7

I have said, **Ye are gods**; and all of you are children of the most High. But ye shall die like men, and fall like one of the princes.

Ephesians 2: 4-7

But God, who is rich in mercy, for his great love wherewith he loved us, Even when we were dead in sins, hath quickened us together with Christ, (by grace ye are saved;) And hath raised us up together, and made us sit together in heavenly places in Christ Jesus: That in the ages to come he might shew the exceeding riches of his grace in his kindness toward us through Christ Jesus.

John 1: 12-13

But as many as received him, to them gave he power to become the sons of God, even to them that believe on his name: Which were born, not of blood, nor of the will of the flesh, nor of the will of man, but of God.

CHAPTER VI
GOD IS FAITHFUL

When you understand the journey of our restoration in Christ, you will then be privileged to grasp a crumb of God's faithfulness. Indeed, God, in His faithfulness, blesses forever, forgives forever, and loves forever. He is truly the Lord. The first space to study the faithfulness of God is in the fact that He has put His Spirit in man since creation (mud, spirit, and soul). Man was corrupted, and the Spirit of God went out of man. But God, in His faithfulness, has designed a plan of redemption to place His Spirit in us. By this act, it's as if the voice of God is saying, "I want you to be my temple." Be my temple. Imagine that God is love and that because of His faithfulness, He loves eternally; God forgives us, and because of His faithfulness, He forgives us eternally; God protects us, and because of His faithfulness, He protects us eternally; and much more.

God does everything He says in His Word and invites us to obedience by doing what He asks of us in His word. We need to master His Word and, above all, not doubt it; therefore, we need to have faith in it.

Faith is the key by which we function with God.

God's promise to Abraham was maintained despite the bad behavior of his descendants because of God's faithfulness.

All those who took the time to build a beautiful relationship with God were able to testify to His fidelity: Daniel, Joshua, Joseph, David, etc. Our turn has now arrived to build our personal relationship with Him and reach this dimension of faith to live and testify to His loyalty. In the meantime, let's think about the sun that rises every morning, the stars that appear every evening, the rain that continues to fall, the wind that still blows, and the plants that continue to provide oxygen and absorb carbon dioxide. These are all expressions of God's faithfulness.

Make sure you understand and believe God's promises and your testimony will be assured.

BIBLICAL REFERENCES

1 John 1: 9

If we confess our sins, he is faithful and just to forgive us our sins, and to cleanse us from all unrighteousness.

2 Thessalonians 3: 3

But the Lord is faithful, who shall stablish you, and keep you from evil.

2 Timothy 2: 11-13

It is a faithful saying: For if we be dead with him, we shall also live with him: If we suffer, we shall also reign with him: if we deny him, he also will deny us: If we believe not, yet he abideth faithful: he cannot deny himself.

Joshua 1: 8-9

This book of the law shall not depart out of thy mouth; but thou shalt meditate therein day and night, that thou mayest observe to do according to all that is written therein: for then thou shalt make thy way prosperous, and then thou shalt have good success. Have not I commanded thee? Be strong and of a good courage; be not afraid, neither be thou dismayed: for the LORD thy God is with thee whithersoever thou goest.

1 Corinthians 6: 17, 19-20

But he that is joined unto the Lord is one spirit. What? Know ye not that your body is the temple of the Holy Ghost which is in you, which ye have of God, and ye are not your own? For ye are bought with a price: therefore glorify God in your body, and in your spirit, which are God's.

1 Corinthians 1: 8-9

Who shall also confirm you unto the end, that ye may be blameless in the day of our Lord Jesus-Christ. God is faithful, by whom ye were called unto the fellowship of his Son Jesus Christ our Lord.

Psalms 36: 5

Thy mercy, O LORD, is in the heavens; and thy faithfulness reacheth unto the clouds.

Jeremiah 1: 12

Then said the LORD unto me, Thou hast well seen: for I will hasten my word to perform it.

John 15: 7

If ye abide in me, and my words abide in you, ye shall ask what ye will, and it shall be done unto you.

Psalms 37: 4

Delight thyself also in the LORD: and he shall give thee the desires of thine heart.

1 John 5:14-15

And this is the confidence that we have in him, that, if we ask any thing according to his will, he heareth us: And if we know that he hear us, whatsoever we ask, we know that we have the petitions that we desired of him.

Matthew 7:7-11

Ask, and it shall be given you; seek, and ye shall find; knock, and it shall be opened unto you: For every one that asketh receiveth; and he that seeketh findeth; and to him that knocketh it shall be opened. Or what man is there of you, whom if his son ask bread, will he give him a stone? Or if he ask a fish, will he give him a serpent? **If ye then, being evil, know how to give good gifts unto your children, how much more shall your Father which is in heaven give good things to them that ask him?**

CHAPTER VII
GOD IS OMNIPOTENT, OMNISCIENT, AND OMNIPRESENT

Omnipresent, omniscient, and omnipotent are three divine attributes that, in my opinion, determine the perfection of God. He can do everything; He knows everything; He is everywhere at all times. He is a wonderful God.

Science does its best to try to explain the marvelous works of God and to make them usable and accessible to human beings, but God remains the master of his creation. Take the time to appreciate the works of creation and the functioning of your heart—a pump that works 24 hours a day. It does not heat up, and you do not put gasoline in it. A tired or poorly functioning heart is the exception that confirms the rule of its perfection. Our lungs are also a perfect example of his work—a device that purifies the air that infiltrates our respiratory system.

Have you ever taken the time to study how a tree works—the symbiosis between the soil, the atmosphere, and the tree—and the intelligent exchanges that they combine on their own? Have you ever thought about the Earth, which remains suspended but functions in a balance that makes it move, which rotates on itself at the same time as it revolves around the sun? When spinning, no one falls into the void, yet the Earth is round and humanity lives on its surface. What a wonderful God we have who loves us!

God is with us every day until the end of the world; He is our shepherd. He watches over every strand of our hair and the nails on our toes.

BIBLICAL REFERENCES

Matthew 28: 16-20

Then the eleven disciples went away into Galilee, into a mountain where Jesus had appointed them. And when they saw him, they worshipped him: but some doubted. And Jesus came and spake unto them, saying, all power is given unto me in heaven and in earth. Go ye therefore, and teach all nations, baptizing them in the name of the Father, and of the Son, and of the Holy Ghost: Teaching them to observe all things whatsoever I have commanded you: and, lo, **I am with you always, even unto the end of the world. Amen.**

Luke 1: 36-38

And, behold, thy cousin Elisabeth, she hath also conceived a son in her old age: and this is the sixth month with her, who was called barren. For with God nothing shall be impossible. And Mary said, Behold the handmaid of the Lord; be it unto me according to thy word. And the angel departed from her.

Mark 10: 23-27

And Jesus looked round about, and saith unto his disciples, How hardly shall they that have riches enter into the kingdom of God! And the disciples were astonished at his words. But Jesus answereth again, and saith unto them, Children, how hard is it for them that trust in riches to enter into the kingdom of God! It is easier for a camel to go through the eye of a needle, than for a rich man to enter into the kingdom of God. And they were astonished out of measure, saying among themselves, Who then can be saved? And Jesus looking upon them saith, With men it is impossible, but not with God: for **with God all things are possible.**

Jeremiah 23: 24

Can any hide himself in secret places that I shall not see him? saith the LORD. Do not I fill heaven and earth? saith the LORD.

Psalm 139: 7-13

Whither shall I go from thy spirit? or whither shall I flee from thy presence? If I ascend up into heaven, thou art there: if I make my bed in hell, behold, thou art there. If I take the wings of the morning, and dwell in the uttermost parts of the sea; Even there shall thy hand lead me, and thy right hand shall hold me. If I say, Surely the darkness shall cover me; even the night shall be light about me. Yea, the darkness hideth not from thee; but the night shineth as the day: the darkness and the light are both alike to thee. For thou hast possessed my reins: thou hast covered me in my mother's womb.

Isaiah 40: 13-14, 26

Who hath directed the Spirit of the LORD, or being his counsellor hath taught him? With whom took he counsel, and who instructed him, and taught him in the path of judgment, and taught him knowledge, and shewed to him the way of understanding? Lift up your eyes on high, and behold who hath created these things, that bringeth out their host by number: he calleth them all by names by the greatness of his might, for that he is strong in power; not one faileth.

Romans 11: 33-34

O the depth of the riches both of the wisdom and knowledge of God! how unsearchable are his judgments, and his ways past finding out! For who hath known the mind of the Lord? or who hath been his counsellor?

Deuteronomy 29: 29

The secret things belong unto the LORD our God: but those things which are revealed belong unto us and to our children forever, that we may do all the words of this law.

CHAPTER VIII

GOD JUST ASKS US TO BELIEVE IN HIM AND IN HIS SON, JESUS

Believe" is a little word that makes such waves in the world and which grants men incredible privileges: salvation, the dimension of sonship, the status of heirs of the divine kingdom and co-heirs of Christ, the temple of God when his Spirit dwells in us, God's authority, grace, an exalted place in Christ, and more. When we believe in God, it means that we have faith in Him, and that is the essential part of what He asks of us: faith.

You cannot serve God without faith, and you cannot believe in God if you do not believe in His Word. He tells us: "My word is the truth," and He is also the truth.

Let's take a moment to study Abraham's journey with God to gain a proper understanding of faith. Do you know who Abraham is? The ancestor of the Hebrew (Jewish) people. When they first met, God told him, "Hey! Abraham, leave your country; I will give you another one." By faith, Abraham left his land, and God gave him the following promise: "This new territory that I am giving you will forever be yours and your descendants." God always fulfills His promises, but do you have the faith to believe His promises like Abraham did?

You cannot criticize God or incriminate Him if you have not already had a relationship with Him or even know His promises for your life. You then have no expectations of God.

My question to you is: What are you afraid of?

- The word believe?
- God himself?
- Expenses that believing can cause?
- The opinion of others (friends, families, colleagues, etc.)?

Think about it!

Friends once asked me this question: "What if God didn't exist?

I told them that on earth, I would have had the privilege of loving, being kind, being patient, and living without illness, with the feeling that all my sins were forgiven. All this only makes me feel good. In addition, I know that **God is much more alive than me** through his Spirit, who lives in me, teaches me, guides me, and consoles me daily.

"Believe on the Lord Jesus and you and your family will be saved."

Know it, dear reader: nature suffers like a woman during childbirth; she is only waiting for the awakening of the sons and daughters of God, including you and me. Do not wait!

Remember, we always believe in something or someone because we are created to believe.

Faith is only the beginning of the walk. When you start living what you believe, it's no longer faith; it's your lifestyle.

BIBLICAL REFERENCES

Hebrews 11: 1

Now faith is the substance of things hoped for, the evidence of things not seen.

Genesis 12: 1-3

Now the LORD had said unto Abram (who became later Abraham), Get thee out of thy country, and from thy kindred, and from thy father's house, unto a land that I will shew thee:

And I will make of thee a great nation, and I will bless thee, and make thy name great; and thou shalt be a blessing:

And I will bless them that bless thee, and curse him that curseth thee: and in thee shall all families of the earth be blessed.

Genesis 15: 1

After these things, the word of the LORD came unto Abram in a vision *(One of God's canal to speak),* saying, Fear not, Abram: I am thy shield, and thy exceeding great reward.

Genesis 13: 14-16

And the LORD said unto Abram, after that Lot was separated from him, Lift up now thine eyes, and look from the place where thou art northward, and southward, and eastward, and westward:

For all the land which thou seest, to thee will I give it, and to thy seed for ever.

And I will make thy seed as the dust of the earth: so that if a man can number the dust of the earth, then shall thy seed also be numbered.

John 1: 12

But as many as received him, to them gave he **power to become the sons of God**, even to them that believe on his name:

Mark 16: 16-20

He that believeth and is baptized shall be saved; but he that believeth not shall be damned.

And these signs shall follow them that believe; In my name shall they cast out devils; they shall speak with new tongues;

They shall take up serpents; and if they drink any deadly thing, it shall not hurt them; they shall lay hands on the sick, and they shall recover.

So then after the Lord had spoken unto them, he was received up into heaven, and sat on the right hand of God.

And they went forth, and preached everywhere, the Lord working with them, and confirming the word with signs following. Amen.

Romans 8: 14-15

For as many as are led by the Spirit of God, they are the sons of God.

For ye have not received the spirit of bondage again to fear; but ye have received the Spirit of adoption, whereby we cry, Abba, Father.

John 16: 7-13

Nevertheless I tell you the truth; It is expedient for you that I go away: for if I go not away, the Comforter will not come unto you; but if I depart, I will send him unto you.

And when he is come, he will reprove the world of sin, and of righteousness, and of judgment:

Of sin, because they believe not on me;

Of righteousness, because I go to my Father, and ye see me no more;

Of judgment, because the prince of this world is judged.

I have yet many things to say unto you, but ye cannot bear them now.

Howbeit when he, the Spirit of truth, is come, he will guide you into all truth: for he shall not speak of himself; but whatsoever he shall hear, that shall he speak: and he will shew you things to come.

Acts 8: 14-17

Now when the apostles which were at Jerusalem heard that Samaria had received the word of God, they sent unto them Peter and John:

Who, when they were come down, prayed for them, that they might receive the Holy Ghost:

(For as yet he was fallen upon none of them: only they were baptized in the name of the Lord Jesus.)

Then laid they their hands on them, and they received the Holy Ghost.

Romans 8: 19-22

For the earnest expectation of the creature waiteth for the manifestation of the sons of God.

For the creature was made subject to vanity, not willingly, but by reason of him who hath subjected the same in hope,

Because the creature itself also shall be delivered from the bondage of corruption into the glorious liberty of the children of God.

For we know that the whole creation groaneth and travaileth in pain together until now.

CHAPTER IX
GOD DOES NOT ACCUSE US

I don't know how many times you have already been told: you are sinners, you are condemned, you are cursed, you are guilty, you are finished. It is very hard to hear these words, often from people who are angry or segregated. But do you know that God's first message to us is, "I love you with an immeasurable love, and I would like you to become my son, my daughter, through my son Jesus"? I invite you to take the time to express your love in this way to someone around you and watch their reaction. To this message of expression of his love, God expects a response that expresses awareness, awakening, recognition, acceptance of oneself and of his love, and the desire to move forward in his plan of life. He is ready to forgive your sins, lighten your heavy burdens, lead you step by step into His truth, and renew you. His Holy Spirit is just waiting for your "YES" to start your new beginning with you.

God gives us grace by concocting a famous plan of redemption to save us: Jesus.

I am here to tell you that yes, I was a sinner, but not anymore, and this grace that I received, which granted me salvation, is knocking on your door too, here and now, on everyone's doorstep. But the question is: you who are reading me right now, what are you going to do with it? Will you receive it as I did and grant yourself, at the same time, the privilege of saying with faith from now on, YES, I WAS, but now I am a new creature, which never existed before, wonderfully and fearfully made? Hallelujah!

Imagine yourself changing your world completely from one second to the next. Imagine being able to say to someone you hurt, "Yes, I did, but now I'm not that person anymore. I received God's grace and it has transformed my life. " May this word be your first testimony in the divine Kingdom. In the name of Jesus!

When you have the choice between wealth and poverty, your current state doesn't matter. The choice you make now after reading my message right away matters because it is the only one that prevails.

BIBLICAL REFERENCES

Romans 6: 20-23

For when ye were the servants of sin, ye were free from righteousness.

What fruit had ye then in those things whereof ye are now ashamed? For the end of those things is death.

But now being made free from sin, and become servants to God, ye have your fruit unto holiness, and the end everlasting life.

For the wages of sin is death; but the gift of God is eternal life through Jesus Christ our Lord.

John 3: 16-18

For God so loved the world, that he gave his only begotten Son, that whosoever believeth in him should not perish, but have everlasting life.

For God sent not his Son into the world to condemn the world; but that the world through him might be saved.

He that believeth on him is not condemned: but he that believeth not is condemned already, because he hath not believed in the name of the only begotten Son of God.

Ephesians 2: 1-9

And you hath he quickened, who were dead in trespasses and sins;

Wherein in time past ye walked according to the course of this world, according to the prince of the power of the air, the spirit that now worketh in the children of disobedience:

Among whom also we all had our conversation in times past in the lusts of our flesh, fulfilling the desires of the flesh and of the mind; and were by nature the children of wrath, even as others.

But God, who is rich in mercy, for his great love wherewith he loved us,

Even when we were dead in sins, hath quickened us together with Christ, (by grace ye are saved;)

And hath raised us up together, and made us sit together in heavenly places in Christ Jesus:

That in the ages to come he might shew the exceeding riches of his grace in his kindness toward us through Christ Jesus.

For by grace are ye saved through faith; and that not of yourselves: it is the gift of God:

Not of works, lest any man should boast.

Hebrews 1: 2-6

God Hath, in these last days, spoken unto us by his Son, whom he hath appointed heir of all things, by whom also he made the worlds;

Who being the brightness of his glory, and the express image of his person, and upholding all things by the word of his power, when **he had by himself purged our sins**, sat down on the right hand of the Majesty on high:

Being made so much better than the angels, as he hath by inheritance obtained a more excellent name than they.

For unto which of the angels said he at any time, Thou art my Son, this day have I begotten thee? And again, I will be to him a Father, and he shall be to me a Son?

And again, when he bringeth in the firstbegotten into the world, he saith, And let all the angels of God worship him.

CHAPTER X
GOD WANTS US TO BE HIS PEOPLE AND LIVE IN UNITY

The first sign indicative of God's presence in a community is love; then comes unity. God is love. The one who produces love in us is the same one who provides for our unity. Love must be properly appreciated according to God's definition to achieve unity. Let us measure ourselves on the scale of love and see to what level love already permeates our hearts.

Our degree of success depends on this scale (like our failures).

The quality of our relationships with others depends on this scale.

Our physical and mental health depends on where we are on this scale.

Our whole life depends on this scale.

The last line of the scale contains all the characteristics of our lives that harm the harmony and balance of things.

God invites us not to leave room in us for these attitudes that the word of God calls fruits of the flesh.

The upper part of the scale contains the characteristics that God wants us to manifest in our daily lives. He puts his Spirit within us for this accomplishment. He encourages us to create a very particular lifestyle for ourselves by engaging in psalms, hymns, and spiritual songs, singing and celebrating the praises of God with all our hearts.

I invite you to create your own love scale. In the last line, cross out the points that are no longer part of your life, italicize the points that you are working on, and leave the points to be worked on as they are. At the top, **put your accomplishments in bold**, items currently being improved in italics, and leave the others as is.

The Scale of Love

Love	*PERFECT LOVE*	Love
	Perseverance	
	Hope	
	Trust	
	Pardon	
	Joy	
	Justice	
	Meekness	
	Humility	
	Collective interest	
	Honesty	
	Kindness	
	Goodness	
	Patience	
Fornication – Impurity – Dissolution – Idolatry – Magic – Enmities – Quarrels – Jealousies – Animosities – Disputes – Divisions – Sects – Envy – Drunkenness – Excessive eating		

A German proverb says: "Love sees roses without thorns."

Furthermore, Jesus himself prayed to the Father that we would be united, as the Father, he, and the Spirit are united. If we possess the love of God, we can also say that our spirit, our soul, and our body are united, knowing that our spirit must be the one who leads. Indeed, God communicates with us through our spirit. It is then essential to command our soul and our body to submit to the authority of our spirit. When this harmony is established, the guilt disappears. Know that prayer is a formidable weapon for obtaining this unity (express your will before the throne of the Almighty). Living without guilt is proof of love. This subject is one of the facts that pushed me to write this book: a community of God united around the shareable essential.

That is why, if you agree with the different ideas shared in this book about God, you are already members of the community of God with me because we believe the same things about our God. That's wonderful!

Division is the worst enemy of the church; this is why our Lord Jesus invites us to support each other instead of causing division within us.

BIBLICAL REFERENCES

Galatians 5: 18, 22-25

But if ye be led of the Spirit, ye are not under the law.

But the fruit of the Spirit is love, joy, peace, longsuffering, gentleness, goodness, faith,

Meekness, temperance: against such there is no law.

And they that are Christ's have crucified the flesh with the affections and lusts.

If we live in the Spirit, let us also walk in the Spirit.

1 Corinthians 13: 4-8

Love suffereth long, and is kind; love envieth not; love vaunteth not itself, is not puffed up,

Doth not behave itself unseemly, seeketh not her own, is not easily provoked, **thinketh no evil**;

Rejoiceth not in iniquity, but rejoiceth in the truth;

Beareth all things, believeth all things, hopeth all things, endureth all things.

Love never faileth.

John 17: 1-3; 9-11; 20-23

These words spake Jesus, and lifted up his eyes to heaven, and said, Father, the hour is come; glorify thy Son, that thy Son also may glorify thee:

As thou hast given him power over all flesh, that he should give eternal life to as many as thou hast given him.

And this is life eternal, that they might know thee the only true God, and Jesus Christ, whom thou hast sent.

I pray for them: I pray not for the world, but for them which thou hast given me; for they are thine.

And all mine are thine, and thine are mine; and I am glorified in them.

And now I am no more in the world, but these are in the world, and I come to thee. Holy Father, **keep through thine own name those whom thou hast given me, that they may be one, as we are.**

Neither pray I for these alone, but for them also which shall believe on me through their word;

That they all may be one; as thou, Father, art in me, and I in thee, that they also may be one in us: that the world may believe that thou hast sent me.

And the glory which thou gavest me I have given them; **that they may be one, even as we are one:**

I in them, and thou in me, that they may be made perfect in one; and that the world may know that thou hast sent me, and hast loved them, as thou hast loved me.

Father, I will that they also, whom thou hast given me, be with me where I am; that they may behold my glory, which thou hast given me: for thou lovedst me before the foundation of the world.

Matthew 18: 19-20

Again I say unto you, that if two of you shall agree on earth as touching anything that they shall ask, it shall be done for them of my Father which is in heaven.

For **where two or three are gathered together in my name, there am I in the midst of them.**

Genesis 11: 1-7

And the whole earth was of one language, and of one speech.

And it came to pass, as they journeyed from the east, that they found a plain in the land of Shinar; and they dwelt there.

And they said one to another, Go to, let us make brick, and burn them thoroughly. And they had brick for stone, and slime had they for morter.

And they said, Go to, let us build us a city and a tower, whose top may reach unto heaven; and let us make us a name, lest we be scattered abroad upon the face of the whole earth.

And the LORD came down to see the city and the tower, which the children of men builded.

And the LORD said, Behold, **the people is one, and they have all one language; and this they begin to do: and**

now nothing will be restrained from them, which they have imagined to do.

Go to, let us go down, and there confound their language, that they may not understand one another's speech.

Colossians 3: 12-17

Put on therefore, as the elect of God, holy and beloved, bowels of mercies, kindness, humbleness of mind, meekness, longsuffering;

Forbearing one another, and forgiving one another, if any man have a quarrel against any: even as Christ forgave you, so also do ye.

And above all these things put on charity, which is the bond of perfectness.

And **let the peace of God rule in your hearts, to the which also ye are called in one body**; and be ye thankful.

Let the word of Christ dwell in you richly in all wisdom; teaching and admonishing one another in psalms and hymns and spiritual songs, singing with grace in your hearts to the Lord.

And whatsoever ye do in word or deed, do all in the name of the Lord Jesus, giving thanks to God and the Father by him.

CHAPTER XI
GOD WANTS US TO DOMINATE IN ALL THINGS

God created us (man) on the sixth day of creation in his image and after his likeness, and there we were given an enormous mission: to dominate, subjugate, and multiply. He also entrusted us with the mission of cultivating and guarding the garden. We can understand from this that dominating is in our nature because it comes to us by order from the Creator. Imagine buying a racing car that has the sole purpose of being able to cook; you would have cried foul. And yet, in straying from our original mission, we typically resemble this car. In some cases today, we can say that yes, men dominate, but without God, who is the master of his work, we then became this racing machine that works without the manufacturer's manual. We, therefore, function like someone who is promoted in a company (the land). The owner of the company (God) appoints him as general manager. Once in office, the manager (the men who dominate) completely sets aside the owner's guidelines, transmits his own standards to the employees (the men who submit to the dominants), and does everything possible to make the owner forget. As a result, some employees seem to be on the verge of forgetting the owner and starting to follow and operate according to the manager's directives. The downside is that the owner is extremely powerful. Crosses (XXXXX), barriers, and lines (-------) only bring it more and more into view because the owner's imprint is everywhere. His image is on the paychecks, and the employees are barely surviving the manager's new laws. Meanwhile, some former employees keep leaking the goodness of how the owner operated when he was in office. Now, employees are hesitating between getting fired while trying to talk to the owner and continuing to endure the operations of the current manager.

The dilemma of today's world.

Some dominant people act without God the Creator; this is why they destroy resources instead of managing them. Today, we are even talking about a global plan to destroy the majority of the world's population, the destruction of the ozone layer, and the need to take measures to become carbon neutral. The dominant ones, being admittedly defeated, invest tirelessly to create another world for them on another planet, accessible only to the dominants. How boring the life of the dominants is without the dominated! Just imagine producing without having consumers consume the production.

God, seated on his celestial throne, observing the dealings of man and seeing the man he created become rather a slave than a dominant one, does not cry foul. He sees that we have lost our way, and he calls us to refocus. He is a God of enormous temperance.

In this call for reframing, God increases man's power by passing him from creature to son, by granting him abundant and more than sufficient grace, and by giving him a place of superiority in Christ, at his right, in the heavenly places. About this place, the word of God specifies: above the dominations, above the authorities, above the powers, above the dignities, and above every name that can be named in this century and in the coming century. When I learned of this revelation, I automatically felt untouchable and indomitable—not after death or when I am in heaven, as some people believe, but now on this earth, I live my daily position as a dominion in Christ. This remains God's call for humanity even today.

We have a place in heavenly places in Christ where God positions us to rule. Let us say it best: Christ is the village in which we dwell, and this village is placed far above all the evils of the world, far above all the riches of the world, far above all the authorities of the world, far above everything. Nature is just waiting for our manifestation.

BIBLICAL REFERENCES

Genesis 1: 26-28

And God said, **Let us make man in our image, after our likeness: and let them have dominion** over the fish of the sea, and over the fowl of the air, and over the cattle, and over all the earth, and over every creeping thing that creepeth upon the earth.

So God created man in his own image, in the image of God created he him; male and female created he them.

And God blessed them, and God said unto them, **Be fruitful, and multiply, and replenish the earth, and subdue it: and have dominion over** the fish of the sea, and over the fowl of the air, and over every living thing that moveth upon the earth.

Genesis 2: 15

And the LORD God took the man, and put him into the garden of Eden to dress it and to keep it.

Ephesians 1: 20-23

Which he wrought in Christ, when he raised him from the dead, and set him at his own right hand in the heavenly places,

Far above all principality, and power, and might, and dominion, and every name that is named, not only in this world, but also in that which is to come:

And hath put all things under his feet, and gave him to be the head over all things to the church,

Which is his body, the fulness of him that filleth all in all.

Ephesians 2: 4-7

But God, who is rich in mercy, for his great love wherewith he loved us,

Even when we were dead in sins, hath quickened us together with Christ, (by grace ye are saved ;)

And *hath raised us up together, and made us sit together in heavenly places in Christ Jesus*:

That in the ages to come he might shew the exceeding riches of his grace in his kindness toward us through Christ Jesus.

Matthew 18: 18

Verily I say unto you, Whatsoever ye shall bind on earth shall be bound in heaven: and whatsoever ye shall loose on earth shall be loosed in heaven.

CHAPTER XII

GOD WANTS US TO RESOLVE OUR CONFLICTS IN LOVE

The spiritual image that appeals to me the most is that of Judah among the twelve disciples of Jesus. Yes, he was there among the twelve, talking among themselves, when Jesus discerned the subject of their conversation and even knew what they were thinking in their hearts. The Lord Jesus also detected what the Pharisees were meditating in their hearts; he walked on water, he healed the sick, he raised the dead, and he was equipped with wisdom known to all. Yet Judah, a thief and a traitor, was there among them during the three years of his ministry, and he never had a single reproach. We could ask ourselves how it is that the Lord could not understand and even foresee Judah's move. The Lord Jesus is the one who had the mission of bringing peace and forgiveness to the world; how can we forgive if we do not suffer harm? The attitude of the Lord Jesus toward Judah clearly shows us what our God expects of us: "If you forgive others, I also forgive you," says the Lord. The Lord had extraordinary patience in putting up with those who hurt Him, and He puts the Holy Spirit within us to produce the love and patience necessary for us to do as He did.

The lesson is huge here, my friends. The Lord has taught us to do things the right way by guiding our steps. This patience to endure pays off; it has led him into his glory. No one has spoken of division in his troop during his time on earth until today. Judah received his verdict, and the Lord received his glory. Hallelujah!

Some will say, "I can't suffer that much for one person." God does not ask us to suffer; he asks us to give him control. He is the God of vengeance. Adonai is his name. Hallelujah!

Before you pull out your reasoning drawer and say you never hope to have such patience, let's look at the results he achieved in his ministry. Fortunately, when our God sends, He provides. He places his Holy Spirit at our entire disposal to produce in us, among other things, patience. You may be wondering, *So why don't I have the patience*? The answer may be that you don't believe you have it, and you often say you don't have patience.

Before talking about yourself, find out what God says about you because he knows you better than you know yourself.

Imagine a world without conflict where harmony reigns, we forgive each other, we help each other, we discuss together even if we meet for the first time, and we trust each other. This is the life that God designed for us. Have you ever heard of a man or woman being arrested because they are too patient, too caring, or too loyal? The apostle

Paul was right when he said, "The law is not against these things."

The Word of God offers us a method of conflict resolution in the rare cases where this happens in the kingdom: Attempt an amicable solution; if necessary, call a witness; if necessary, talk to the church; and if necessary, see them as pagans.

BIBLICAL REFERENCES

John 6: 63-65

It is the spirit that quickeneth; the flesh profiteth nothing: the words that I speak unto you, they are spirit, and they are life.

But there are some of you that believe not. For *Jesus knew from the beginning who they were that believed not, and who should betray him.*

And he said, Therefore said I unto you, that no man can come unto me, except it were given unto him of my Father.

Matthew 9: 2-6

And, behold, they brought to him a man sick of the palsy, lying on a bed: and Jesus seeing their faith said unto the sick of the palsy; Son, be of good cheer; thy sins be forgiven thee.

And, behold, certain of the scribes said within themselves, This man blasphemeth.

And *Jesus knowing their thoughts* said, Wherefore think ye evil in your hearts?

For whether is easier, to say, Thy sins be forgiven thee; or to say, Arise, and walk?

But that ye may know that the Son of man hath power on earth to forgive sins, (then saith he to the sick of the palsy,) Arise, take up thy bed, and go unto thine house.

Matthew 18: 15-17

Moreover if thy brother shall trespass against thee, go and tell him his fault between thee and him alone: if he shall hear thee, thou hast gained thy brother.

But if he will not hear thee, then take with thee one or two more, that in the mouth of two or three witnesses every word may be established.

And if he shall neglect to hear them, tell it unto the church: but if he neglect to hear the church, let him be unto thee as an heathen man and a publican.

Galatians 5: 22-23

But the fruit of the Spirit is love, joy, peace, longsuffering, gentleness, goodness, faith,

Meekness, temperance: *against such there is no law*.

Psalms 94: 1, 22-23

O Lord God, to whom vengeance belongeth; O God, to whom vengeance belongeth, shew thyself.

But the LORD is my defence; and my God is the rock of my refuge.

And he shall bring upon them their own iniquity, and shall cut them off in their own wickedness; yea, the LORD our God shall cut them off.

Philippians 1: 27-30

Only let your conversation be as it becometh the gospel of Christ: that whether I come and see you, or else be absent, I may hear of your affairs, that ye stand fast in one spirit, with one mind striving together for the faith of the gospel;

And in nothing terrified by your adversaries: which is to them an evident token of perdition, but to you of salvation, and that of God.

For unto you it is given in the behalf of Christ, **not only to believe on him, but also to suffer for his sake;**

Having the same conflict which ye saw in me, and now hear to be in me.

James 1: 2-4

My brethren, count it all joy when ye fall into divers temptations;

Knowing this, that the trying of your faith worketh patience.

But let patience have her perfect work, that ye may be perfect and entire, wanting nothing.

Matthew 5: 9-12

Blessed are the peacemakers: for they shall be called the children of God.

Blessed are they which are persecuted for righteousness' sake: for theirs is the kingdom of heaven.

Blessed are ye, when men shall revile you, and persecute you, and shall say all manner of evil against you falsely, for my sake.

Rejoice, and be exceeding glad: for great is your reward in heaven: for so persecuted they the prophets which were before you.

Matthew 6: 9-13

After this manner therefore pray ye: Our Father which art in heaven, Hallowed be thy name.

Thy kingdom come, Thy will be done in earth, as it is in heaven.

Give us this day our daily bread.

And forgive us our debts, as we forgive our debtors.

And lead us not into temptation, but deliver us from evil: For thine is the kingdom, and the power, and the glory, forever. Amen.

CHAPTER XIII
GOD WANTS US TO BE FREE

Let me take a moment to remind you that God's plan for man since creation is dominion (Genesis 1:26-28). It is very important not to lose sight of this fact (it is not information), and I would like to point out again that our mission of domination is a fact. Let's say we failed the first time—because maybe it was too good to be true, but I tell you again today, God cannot lie (Numbers 23:19), but your doubt can lie to you.

I also spoke to you earlier about this second plan of salvation that God designed for humanity with Jesus, even giving us a promotion by passing us from creature to son, depositing his Spirit in us and making us sit in places heavenly in Christ above all things that would harm us, and the most beautiful and complete of all, in giving us grace (John 1:12-13; Ephesians 2:4-7; Romans 6: 3-3, 14).

Since the implementation of this plan of redemption, God no longer deals directly with man but through Christ and his Spirit, who lives in man. He looks at us, saves us, and treats us through Christ, who serves as our savior (filter) by dying on the cross for our sins and thereby freeing us from the wages of death.

Freedom is a beautiful word, and it is even more beautiful in God's dictionary. Christ's main mission was to give us freedom because we have been slaves to sin, slaves to the law, and it seems that even today, we persist in being slaves to modernity, to culture, to what we would say about it, about fashion, et cetera. God has called us to dominate, but we persist in allowing ourselves to be dominated to the point of becoming slaves. Have you noticed that God sent his only Son to free us from the slavery of sin? He offers us the freedom to fully live out his plan for our lives (Luke 4:16–21; Galatians 5:1; Romans 8:1-2).

The Bible records that God said to the prophet Jeremiah, "I know the plans I have for you, plans of peace so that you will have a future and hope." He also said to Joshua, "Keep my word, and you will succeed in all your endeavors." He also spoke to the apostle Paul on the road to Damascus, and he also spoke to me. He has a word of freedom for you too. Come to him and listen to what he has to say to you. Stay blessed!

BIBLICAL REFERENCES

Genesis 1: 26-28

And God said, Let us make man in our image, after our likeness: and let them have dominion over the fish of the sea, and over the fowl of the air, and over the cattle, and over all the earth, and over every creeping thing that creepeth upon the earth.

So God created man in his own image, in the image of God created he him; male and female created he them.

And God blessed them, and God said unto them, be fruitful, and multiply, and *replenish the earth, and subdue it: and have dominion over the fish of the sea, and over the fowl of the air, and over every living thing that moveth upon the earth*.

Numbers 23: 19

God is not a man that he should lie; neither the son of man that he should repent: hath he said, and shall he not do it? Or hath he spoken, and shall he not make it good?

John 1: 12-13

But as many as received him, to them gave he power to become the sons of God, even to them that believe on his name:

Which were born, not of blood, nor of the will of the flesh, nor of the will of man, but of God.

Ephesians 2: 4-7

But God, who is rich in mercy, for his great love wherewith he loved us,

Even when we were dead in sins, hath quickened us together with Christ, (by grace ye are saved) And hath raised us up together, and made us sit together in heavenly places in Christ Jesus: That in the ages to come he might shew the exceeding riches of his grace in his kindness toward us through Christ Jesus.

Romans 6: 3-4, 14

Know ye not, that so many of us as were baptized into Jesus Christ were baptized into his death?

Therefore we are buried with him by baptism into death: that like as Christ was raised up from the dead by the glory of the Father, even so we also should walk in newness of life.

For sin shall not have dominion over you: for ye are not under the law, but under grace.

Luke 4: 16-21

And he came to Nazareth, where he had been brought up: and, as his custom was, he went into the synagogue on the sabbath day, and stood up for to read.

And there was delivered unto him the book of the prophet Esaias. And when he had opened the book, he found the place where it was written,

The Spirit of the Lord is upon me, because he hath anointed me to preach the gospel to the poor; he hath sent me to heal the brokenhearted, to preach deliverance to the captives, and recovering of sight to the blind, to set at liberty them that are bruised,

To preach the acceptable year of the Lord.

And he closed the book, and he gave it again to the minister, and sat down. And the eyes of all them that were in the synagogue were fastened on him.

And he began to say unto them, This day is this scripture fulfilled in your ears.

Galatians 5: 1

Stand fast therefore in the liberty wherewith Christ hath made us free, and be not entangled again with the yoke of bondage.

Romans 8: 1-2

There is therefore now no condemnation to them which are in Christ Jesus, who walk not after the flesh, but after the Spirit.

For the law of the Spirit of life in Christ Jesus hath made me free from the law of sin and death.

Luke 4: 14, 17-19

And Jesus returned in the power of the Spirit into Galilee: and there went out a fame of him through all the region round about.

And there was delivered unto him the book of the prophet Esaias. And when he had opened the book, he found the place where it was written,

The Spirit of the Lord is upon me, because he hath anointed me to preach the gospel to the poor; he hath sent me to heal the brokenhearted, to preach deliverance to the captives, and recovering of sight to the blind, to set at liberty them that are bruised,

To preach the acceptable year of the Lord.

Revelation 1: 5-6

And from Jesus Christ, who is the faithful witness, and the first begotten of the dead, and the prince of the kings of the earth. Unto him that loved us, and washed us from our sins in his own blood,

And hath made us kings and priests unto God and his Father; to him be glory and dominion for ever and ever. Amen.

Jeremiah 29: 10-13

For thus saith the Lord, That after seventy years be accomplished at Babylon I will visit you, and perform my good word toward you, in causing you to return to this place.

For I know the thoughts that I think toward you, saith the Lord, thoughts of peace, and not of evil, to give you an expected end.

Then shall ye call upon me, and ye shall go and pray unto me, and I will hearken unto you.

And ye shall seek me, and find me, when ye shall search for me with all your heart.

Jeremiah 1: 4-8

Then the word of the LORD came unto me, saying,

Before I formed thee in the belly I knew thee; and before thou camest forth out of the womb I sanctified thee, and I ordained thee a prophet unto the nations.

Then said I, Ah, Lord GOD! Behold, I cannot speak: for I am a child.

But the LORD said unto me, Say not, I am a child: for thou shalt go to all that I shall send thee, and whatsoever I command thee thou shalt speak.

Be not afraid of their faces: for I am with thee to deliver thee, saith the LORD.

Matthew 11: 28-30

Come unto me, all ye that labour and are heavy laden, and I will give you rest.

Take my yoke upon you, and learn of me; for I am meek and lowly in heart: and ye shall find rest unto your souls.

For my yoke is easy, and my burden is light.

CHAPTER XIV
GOD GIVES US LIFE, HEALTH, AND LIGHT

I bring you excellent news: life is our brother, and our Father is the giver of life. We live in life. We grow in life. Some readers will say, "Wow! Lots of repetitions," and they will get the better of me. But I do not ignore the repetitions; I have fun enjoying the life of God in me by writing these lines, while hoping that you will do the same by reading them. Dear readers, we have been adopted by God to have life, and in receiving this life, we receive health, peace, and much more (John 10:7–11). Never forget that faith is our weapon to grasp all the wonders and promises of God.

I told you earlier that the most beautiful and complete of all the wonders of God is grace. Indeed, it covers all our gaps without leaving a gap—that is to say, perfectly.

Here is the technical sheet: I acknowledge, by faith, that Christ is the savior whom God sent to save mankind; I accept, by baptism, that I died with Christ to sin and that I am resurrected with him, for he has overcome death; I firmly believe that from now on, I receive the Spirit of God who lives in me, and I live in Christ who sits at the right hand of the Father in the heavenly places above all principalities, dominions, authorities, powers, dignities, and every name that can be named in this century and in the century to come (John 1:12–13; Ephesians 2:4–7; Ephesians 1:20–23).

The Spirit of God then became an integral part of my life with the mission to produce fruit worthy of God, which is love, as well as its attributes, to teach me, to console me, to guide me, to intercede in my favor, and to have in me gifts that he judges necessary for the accomplishment of God's plans in my life (John 14:25–26; Romans 8:12–14, 24-27; Galatians 5:22; 1 Corinthians 12:4–11).

In the attributes of love is peace, and furthermore, the Word of God clearly tells us that Jesus gives us peace, his peace (John 14:1, 27).

The Word also tells us that by the stripes of Christ, we are healed (Isaiah 53:5). I have grasped this revelation, which I find revolutionary for my life. Whatever concerns your life, ask yourself two small questions:

1. Did God give it to me? If it's a yes, glorify the Lord; if it's a no, ask yourself the second question:
2. Does he have a name? Yes, and it's a yes because everything that exists has a name. So remember that God places you in Christ above all names, present and future.

This is why it is necessary to know everything that God gives you in his Word. They are as real as a cashier's check or any property. Through your faith, you will bring them back into existence in your life.

Psalms 119:130 tells us: "The entrance of your word gives light"; Psalms 27:1 says: "The LORD is my light and my salvation," knowing that God is His word, which itself is light. This light shines in the darkest moments of life. Our Lord Jesus, in Matthew 5:14, tells us clearly: "You are the light of the world"; in verse 16, he declares: "Let your light shine before men so that they may see your good works." If you see a lack of compassion and expression of good works in the world, tell yourself that the world needs light—the light that God wants us to be. This light is there to bring happiness into our lives.

BIBLICAL REFERENCES

John 10: 7-11

Then said Jesus unto them again, Verily, verily, I say unto you, I am the door of the sheep.

All that ever came before me are thieves and robbers: but the sheep did not hear them.

I am the door: by me if any man enter in, he shall be saved, and shall go in and out, and find pasture.

The thief cometh not, but for to steal, and to kill, and to destroy: **I am come that they might have life, and that they might have it more abundantly.**

I am the good shepherd: **the good shepherd giveth his life for the sheep.**

Galatians 5: 22-23

But the fruit of the Spirit is love, joy, peace, longsuffering, gentleness, goodness, faith,

Meekness, temperance: against such there is no law.

John 14: 25-27

These things have I spoken unto you, being yet present with you.

But the Comforter, which is the Holy Ghost, whom the Father will send in my name, he shall teach you all things, and bring all things to your remembrance, whatsoever I have said unto you.

Peace I leave with you, my peace I give unto you: not as the world giveth, give I unto you. Let not your heart be troubled, neither let it be afraid.

Romans 8: 12-14, 24-27

Therefore, brethren, we are debtors, not to the flesh, to live after the flesh.

For if ye live after the flesh, ye shall die: but if ye through the Spirit do mortify the deeds of the body, ye shall live.

For as many as are led by the Spirit of God, they are the sons of God.

For we are saved by hope: but hope that is seen is not hope: for what a man seeth, why doth he yet hope for?

But if we hope for that we see not, then do we with patience wait for it.

Likewise the Spirit also helpeth our infirmities: for we know not what we should pray for as we ought: but **the Spirit itself maketh intercession for us with groanings which cannot be uttered**.

And he that searcheth the hearts knoweth what is the mind of the Spirit, because he maketh intercession for the saints according to the will of God.

Genesis 2: 7

And the LORD God formed man of the dust of the ground, and breathed into his nostrils the breath of life; and man became a living soul.

Deuteronomy 32: 39

See now that I, even I, am he, and there is no god with me: I kill, and I make alive; I wound, and I heal: neither is there any that can deliver out of my hand.

1 Corinthians 12: 4-11

Now there are diversities of gifts, but the same Spirit.

And there are differences of administrations, but the same Lord.

And there are diversities of operations, but it is the same God which worketh all in all.

But the manifestation of the Spirit is given to every man to profit withal.

For to one is given by the Spirit the word of wisdom; to another the word of knowledge by the same Spirit;

To another faith by the same Spirit; to another the gifts of healing by the same Spirit;

To another the working of miracles; to another prophecy; to another discerning of spirits; to another divers kinds of tongues; to another the interpretation of tongues:

But all these worketh that one and the selfsame Spirit, dividing to every man severally as he will.

John 1: 3-4

All things were made by him; and without him was not anything made that was made.

In him was life; and the life was the light of men.

Nehemiah 9: 6

Thou, even thou, art LORD alone; thou hast made heaven, the heaven of heavens, with all their host, the earth, and all things that are therein, the seas, and all that is therein, and thou preservest them all; and the host of heaven worshippeth thee.

Acts 17: 24-25

God that made the world and all things therein, seeing that he is Lord of heaven and earth, dwelleth not in temples made with hands;

Neither is worshipped with men's hands, as though he needed anything, seeing he giveth to all life, and breath, and all things.

1 Peter 2: 21-24

For even hereunto were ye called: because Christ also suffered for us, leaving us an example, that ye should follow his steps:

Who did no sin, neither was guile found in his mouth:

Who, when he was reviled, reviled not again; when he suffered, he threatened not; but committed himself to him that judgeth righteously:

Who his own self bare our sins in his own body on the tree, that we, being dead to sins, should live unto righteousness: by whose stripes ye were healed.

1 Corinthians 6: 19-20

What? Know ye not that your body is the temple of the Holy Ghost which is in you, which ye have of God, and ye are not your own?

For ye are bought with a price: therefore glorify God in your body, and in *your spirit, which are God's.*

Isaiah 53: 5

But he was wounded for our transgressions, he was bruised for our iniquities: the chastisement of our peace was upon him; and with his stripes we are healed.

Matthew 16: 17-18

And these signs shall follow them that believe; In my name shall they cast out devils; they shall speak with new tongues;

They shall take up serpents; and if they drink any deadly thing, it shall not hurt them; they shall lay hands on the sick, and they shall recover.

John 14: 1, 27

Let not your heart be troubled: ye believe in God, believe also in me. Peace I leave with you, my peace I give unto you: not as the world giveth, give I unto you. Let not your heart be troubled, neither let it be afraid.

Ephesians 1: 3-6

Blessed be the God and Father of our Lord Jesus Christ, who hath blessed us with all spiritual blessings in heavenly places in Christ:

According as he hath chosen us in him before the foundation of the world, that we should be holy and without blame before him in love:

Having predestinated us unto the adoption of children by Jesus Christ to himself, according to the good pleasure of his will,

To the praise of the glory of his grace, wherein he hath made us accepted in the beloved.

CHAPTER XV
GOD LIVES IN US

I always asked myself why God put the will in man since, because of it, we manage to serve God or not to serve Him. The answer I received was that God is not an executioner and that, in creating man, He intended to create another version of Himself: a free being (Genesis 1:27).

Once man has sinned and God has understood that His Spirit will not remain in man (Genesis 6:3), He sets in motion His plan B, the plan for the redemption of humanity, which appeals to the will of man for its implementation (John 1:12–13). Once the will is manifested, God puts His Spirit in man to teach him, to console him, to convince him, to guide him, and to produce in him the fruit of the Spirit, which is the identity of God in him (Galatians 5:22–23). The Holy Spirit is the seal that identifies us with Christ (2 Corinthians 1:21-22).

You may be wondering right now what the relationship is between the Spirit, Christ, and God. Remember, I told you that God created us in His image and likeness (Genesis 1:27). I will reveal to you two other truths from God's Word:

1. The person of God is tripartite. God (the Father), Jesus (the Son who became Christ), and the Holy Spirit who makes the links between God and us. This is why many congregations talk about the trinity of God. God, wanting to dwell in us, uses His Spirit, and we have become the house of the Spirit of God and, therefore, the house of God. Jesus described it so well in his priestly prayer (John 17:22–23).

2. We, being born in the likeness of God, are also tripartite. However, each of the parts has its place: we are spiritual beings (since we are sons of God and God is Spirit), we live in a body, and we have a soul. The apostle Paul understood this well when he spoke of this earthly body that we all have and the heavenly body that awaits us all according to our hope (1 Corinthians 15:35–46).

The problem remains and remains in our consciousness, although its state makes no difference to our responsibility. One piece of law that shocked me the first time I heard it: "No one is supposed to ignore the law." It seems like these six little words are in every law in every country. For example, if you drink alcohol and become drunk, then, while drunk, you decide to drive your car, you can easily be involved in an accident, destroying your life or that of other innocent people. But do you know that when the police go to the scene of the accident, they will not exonerate you by saying, "It's not their fault; he/she was drunk; he/she didn't have all his conscience." On the contrary, the police will tell you that you should not have driven while drunk.

I remember once praying for the power of God to manifest in me. One day, I went to church, and as I entered the courtyard, I met one of the ladies of the church. I touched her head as I greeted her, and I said to her, "Your hair is very beautiful." After the service, this lady came to see me, and, approaching me, she said, "Wow! There is something very powerful in you. This morning, I had a strong migraine, and I even intended not to come to church. But thinking that perhaps my healing is in church, I came anyway. Then you greeted me at the entrance by touching my head, and at that very moment, the migraine disappeared." I shuddered and praised and thanked God, but I had no awareness that this was an answer to my prayer. That was in 2019. One day in 2021, two years later, as I continued to pray to God for power, the Holy Spirit opened my eyes to this 2019 event, and that's when I understood that God has long concluded this matter of power. My shock was great that day, and I asked God for forgiveness for having ignored Him for so long. I love God unfailingly, but when I see the gospel preached without any power, I am ashamed of the church. This is a model that does not exist in the Bible.

I tell you all this to tell you that your conscience deserves an adjustment. Are you aware that the whole person of the Creator of the universe at this moment dwells either within you (if you have already accepted Christ as your Lord) or at the door of your consciousness, saying to you, "Please, let me in." If you are not aware of it, you will never know it, but the truth does not change anything. Think about it!

BIBLICAL REFERENCES

Genesis 1: 27

So God created man in his own image, in the image of God created he him; male and female created he them.

Genesis 6: 3

And the LORD said, My spirit shall not always strive with man, for that he also is flesh: yet his days shall be an hundred and twenty years.

John 1: 12-13

But as many as received him, to them gave he power to become the sons of God, even to them that believe on his name:
Which were born, not of blood, nor of the will of the flesh, nor of the will of man, but of God.

1 Corinthians 6: 19-20

What? Know ye not that *your body is the temple of the Holy Ghost which is in you*, which ye have of God, and ye are not your own?

For ye are bought with a price: therefore glorify God in your body, and *in your spirit, which are God's.*

Ezekiel 36: 27

And *I will put my spirit within you*, and cause you to walk in my statutes, and ye shall keep my judgments, and do them.

2 Corinthians 1: 21-22

Now he which establisheth us with you in Christ, and hath anointed us, is God;

Who hath also sealed us, and given *the earnest of the Spirit in our hearts.*

Romans 8: 11

But if the Spirit of him that raised up Jesus from the dead dwell in you, he that raised up Christ from the dead shall also quicken your mortal bodies by his Spirit that dwelleth in you.

Romans 8: 9

But ye are not in the flesh, but in the Spirit, if so be that the Spirit of God dwell in you. Now if any man have not the Spirit of Christ, he is none of his.

John 17: 22-23

And the glory which thou gavest me I have given them; that they may be one, even as we are one:

I in them, and thou in me, that they may be made perfect in one; and that the world may know that thou hast sent me, and hast loved them, as thou hast loved me.

1 Corinthians 15: 35-46

But some man will say, How are the dead raised up? And with what body do they come?

Thou fool, that which thou sowest is not quickened, except it die:

And that which thou sowest, thou sowest not that body that shall be, but bare grain, it may chance of wheat, or of some other grain: But God giveth it a body as it hath pleased him, and to every seed his own body.

All flesh is not the same flesh: but there is one kind of flesh of men, another flesh of beasts, another of fishes, and another of birds. There are also celestial bodies, and bodies terrestrial: but the glory of the celestial is one, and the glory of the terrestrial is another.

There is one glory of the sun, and another glory of the moon, and another glory of the stars: for one star differeth from another star in glory.

So also is the resurrection of the dead. It is sown in corruption; it is raised in incorruption:

It is sown in dishonour; it is raised in glory: it is sown in weakness; it is raised in power:

It is sown a natural body; it is raised a spiritual body. There is a natural body, and there is a spiritual body.

And so it is written, the first man Adam was made a living soul; the last Adam was made a quickening spirit. Howbeit that was not first which is spiritual, but that which is natural; and afterward that which is spiritual.

1 John 4: 12

No man hath seen God at any time. If we love one another, **God dwelleth in us**, and his love is perfected in us.

John 14: 26

But the Comforter, which is the Holy Ghost, whom the Father will send in my name, he shall teach you all things, and bring all things to your remembrance, whatsoever I have said unto you.

CHAPTER XVI

GOD GIVES US HIS LOVE, HIS JOY, HIS PEACE

I spoke to you in the previous chapter about the Spirit of God, who dwells in us and who is the seal that identifies us with him (Romans 8:9). I so love this word from the Lord of hosts, from the Creator of the universe, from the Almighty, from the Holy One of Israel, who says to each of us, "You are mine" (Isaiah 43:1-4). It's extraordinary!

However, this seal is not ordinary but is alive. It is God in us and has the responsibility to work in us to produce fruit worthy of God: love, as well as its attributes: joy, peace, patience, faithfulness, kindness, temperance, etc. (Galatians 5:22-23).

We are talking here about Love, Joy, and Peace, but God gives us much more than that. Indeed, God is love (1 John 4:7-8). If we are sons and daughters of God created in his image and likeness, we are also called to be love.

Love is a word that we hear a lot around us, but what is the definition of this love that the world talks about so much?

In God's dictionary, love is the ability to be patient, kind, kind, honest, true, just, emphatic, forgiving in all, believing in all, hoping for in all, enduring in all. And to be thus continually and indefinitely (1 Corinthians 13:4-7). Do you think that the love we hear so often around us faithfully meets this definition?

The love that the Holy Spirit produces in us is a very special type that should not be confused with any feeling, often fleeting and which hurts mercilessly in its time. The world makes destructive use of the word Love.

You may be saying to yourself, "I'll never get there!" And you're right—it's the same for me, and God knows it. This is why he puts his Spirit in us to produce this love. Do you want it? If so, I invite you to do two little things:

1. Make love your main prayer request to God: "Lord, I want to possess your love in me; fill me with your love in Jesus' name."

2. Given the place that love is called to occupy in us, this request must be perpetual, constantly seeking the love of God in our lives. Take time to praise God for His wonders so you can strengthen the presence of the Holy Spirit within you. God commands us to fill ourselves with his Spirit by speaking to ourselves in psalms, hymns, and spiritual songs (Ephesians 5:18-20).

God also gives us joy and wants us to be joyful always (1 Thessalonians 5:16). What I want to tell you here is crucial. If you are in Christ and one day or at any time of any day, you find yourself deprived of your joy, consider yourself a person who accidentally loses his way or his place and quickly pulls himself together. Do not give anything or anyone the right to deprive you of what God gives you a right to. The joy of God is our strength (Nehemiah 8:10), and we have this joy within us as soon as the Spirit of God indwells us (Galatians 4:22-23). We also have the presence of the Holy Spirit that produces this joy in us. We need it to overcome all the obstacles, all the circumstances that await our journey and we will have our victory with the fullness of the Holy Spirit in us. We are more than victorious. Hallelujah!

God also gives us his peace (John 14:27) and asks us not to be troubled by what is happening around us: "Believe in God and believe in me" (John 14:1). The Lord is our Shepherd. He cares for us, and it is now up to us to respond to his request: "Believe in God and believe in me."

BIBLICAL REFERENCES

Isaiah 43: 1-4

But now thus saith the LORD that created thee, O Jacob, and he that formed thee, O Israel, Fear not: for I have redeemed thee, I have called thee by thy name; thou art mine.

When thou passest through the waters, I will be with thee; and through the rivers, they shall not overflow thee: when thou walkest through the fire, thou shalt not be burned; neither shall the flame kindle upon thee.

For I am the LORD thy God, the Holy One of Israel, thy Saviour: I gave Egypt for thy ransom, Ethiopia and Seba for thee.

Since thou wast precious in my sight, thou hast been honourable, and I have loved thee: therefore will I give men for thee, and people for thy life.

Galatians 5: 16, 22-23

This I say then, Walk in the Spirit, and ye shall not fulfil the lust of the flesh.

But the fruit of the Spirit is love, joy, peace, longsuffering, gentleness, goodness, faith,

Meekness, temperance: against such there is no law.

1 Corinthians 13: 4-8a

Love suffereth long, and is kind; Love envieth not; Love vaunteth not itself, is not puffed up,

Doth not behave itself unseemly, seeketh not her own, is not easily provoked, thinketh no evil;

Rejoiceth not in iniquity, but rejoiceth in the truth;

Beareth all things, believeth all things, hopeth all things, endureth all things.

Love never faileth.

1 John 4: 7-8

Beloved, let us love one another: *for love is of God*; and every one that loveth is born of God, and knoweth God.

He that loveth not knoweth not God; *for God is love*.

Ephesians 5: 18-21

And be not drunk with wine, wherein is excess; but be filled with the Spirit;

Speaking to yourselves in psalms and hymns and spiritual songs, singing and making melody in your heart to the Lord;

Giving thanks always for all things unto God and the Father in the name of our Lord Jesus Christ;

Submitting yourselves one to another in the fear of God.

1 Thessalonians 5: 12- 24

And we beseech you, brethren, to know them which labour among you, and are over you in the Lord, and admonish you;

And to esteem them very highly in love for their work's sake. And be at peace among yourselves.

Now we exhort you, brethren, warn them that are unruly, comfort the feebleminded, support the weak, be patient toward all men.

See that none render evil for evil unto any man; but ever follow that which is good, both among yourselves, and to all men.

Rejoice evermore.

Pray without ceasing.

In every thing give thanks: for this is the will of God in Christ Jesus concerning you.

Quench not the Spirit.

Despise not prophesyings.

Prove all things; hold fast that which is good.

Abstain from all appearance of evil.

And the very God of peace sanctify you wholly; and I pray God your whole spirit and soul and body be preserved blameless unto the coming of our Lord Jesus Christ.

Faithful is he that calleth you, who also will do it.

Nehemiah 8: 9-11

And Nehemiah, which is the Tirshatha, and Ezra the priest the scribe, and the Levites that taught the people, said unto all the people, This day is holy unto the LORD your God; mourn not, nor weep. For all the people wept, when they heard the words of the law.

Then he said unto them, Go your way, eat the fat, and drink the sweet, and send portions unto them for whom nothing is prepared: for this day is holy unto our LORD: neither be ye sorry; *for the joy of the LORD is your strength.*

So the Levites stilled all the people, saying, *hold your peace*, for the day is holy; neither be ye grieved.

John 14: 1, 25-27

Let not your heart be troubled: ye believe in God, believe also in me.

These things have I spoken unto you, being yet present with you.

But the Comforter, which is the Holy Ghost, whom the Father will send in my name, he shall teach you all things, and bring all things to your remembrance, whatsoever I have said unto you.

Peace I leave with you, my peace I give unto you: not as the world giveth, give I unto you. Let not your heart be troubled, neither let it be afraid.

Romans 8: 35-39

Who shall separate us from the love of Christ? Shall tribulation, or distress, or persecution, or famine, or nakedness, or peril, or sword?

As it is written, For thy sake we are killed all the day long; we are accounted as sheep for the slaughter.

Nay, in all these things *we are more than conquerors through him that loved us.*

For I am persuaded, that neither death, nor life, nor angels, nor principalities, nor powers, nor things present, nor things to come,

Nor height, nor depth, nor any other creature, shall be able to separate us from the love of God, which is in Christ Jesus our Lord.

CHAPTER XVII

GOD GIVES US WISDOM, KNOWLEDGE, AND UNDERSTANDING

God once appeared to King Solomon and asked him, "What do you want me to do for you?" Solomon replied, "I want wisdom and understanding to rule your people."

God was pleased with the response of the king, who was more concerned about God's work than himself. And God said to him, "I will give you what you ask, and I will grant you riches and glory." Wow! I dedicated the year 2023 to my life, my family, and the community of God: "the year of wisdom, intelligence, and knowledge," and I prayed to God during the year that it would develop in us the love of his Word because I understood that word, wisdom, and intelligence are linked, as well as knowledge.

Furthermore, I realized that everything has a beginning, and the Word of God tells us that the beginning of everything is wisdom (Proverbs 3:19–20) and that he founded the earth with wisdom.

God wants us to have wisdom. The apostle James presents the process of gaining wisdom as a truly simple thing: "If anyone lacks wisdom, let him ask God in faith" (James 1:4-5). Do you need wisdom? Yes, you need it. God himself needed it to accomplish the work of creation. Jesus was filled with wisdom, as the prophet Isaiah tells us (Isaiah 11:2). Let's look at a snippet of God's Word that took me a while to understand: I have not given you a spirit of fear, but of wisdom, love, and confidence (2 Timothy 2:6-7). I had spent time questioning God about this text, saying, "But Lord, the opposite of fear is maybe just boldness, so what do love and wisdom have to do with it?" When I received the response from the Holy Spirit, it was so uplifting.

Our fear comes from what we don't know (our ignorance) and what we don't do (our lack of love). Love is the basis. When we practice love, we expect to receive love in return. Let's look at children; they are not afraid of anything because they only know good. As for wisdom, it is the ability to know what I am entitled to and to place everything in its right place. If you believed that God is full of power, authority, and strength and were certain that He watches over you, you would not have been shaken for anything in the world. Indeed, even today, some people find their assurance in the fact that they have a parent with a certain governmental authority in their country and therefore feel untouchable. However, these may be countries that are very little known in the world.

Wisdom, knowledge, and intelligence go hand in hand. One needs the other for its improvement. Jesus was twelve years old when he found himself among the great teachers of the law in Jerusalem. He asked so many relevant questions among these greats of his time that they wanted to know with pride whose son he was. The prophet Isaiah tells us that, yes, Jesus possessed, like our Father, wisdom, knowledge, and intelligence. Pray for wisdom, knowledge, and understanding. Love God and His Word, spend time in His Word to acquire knowledge, and, as a result, develop a good relationship with Him to build the basis of your success.

BIBLICAL REFERENCES

Proverbs 3: 19-20

The LORD by *wisdom* hath founded the earth; by *understanding* hath he established the heavens.

By his *knowledge* the depths are broken up, and the clouds drop down the dew.

James 1: 5-8

If any of you lack wisdom, let him ask of God, that giveth to all men liberally, and upbraideth not; and it shall be given him.

But let him ask in faith, nothing wavering. For he that wavereth is like a wave of the sea driven with the wind and tossed.

For let not that man think that he shall receive any thing of the Lord.

A double minded man is unstable in all his ways.

Isaiah 11: 1-4

And there shall come forth a rod out of the stem of Jesse, and a Branch shall grow out of his roots:

And the spirit of the LORD shall rest upon him, *the spirit of wisdom and understanding, the spirit of counsel and might, the spirit of knowledge and of the fear of the LORD;*

And shall make him of quick understanding in the fear of the LORD: and he shall not judge after the sight of his eyes, neither reprove after the hearing of his ears:

But with righteousness shall he judge the poor, and reprove with equity for the meek of the earth: and he shall smite the earth: with the rod of his mouth, and with the breath of his lips shall he slay the wicked.

2 Timothy 1: 6-7

Wherefore I put thee in remembrance that thou stir up the gift of God, which is in thee by the putting on of my hands.

For God hath not given us the spirit of fear; but of power, and of love, and of *a sound mind*.

Proverbs 9: 10

The fear of the LORD is the beginning of wisdom: and the knowledge of the holy is understanding

Proverbs 4: 6-7

Forsake her not, and she shall preserve thee: love her, and she shall keep thee.

Wisdom is the principal thing; therefore get wisdom: and with all thy getting get understanding.

Ecclesiastes 2:26

For God giveth to a man that is good in his sight wisdom, and knowledge, and joy: but to the sinner he giveth travail, to gather and to heap up, that he may give to him that is good before God. This also is vanity and vexation of spirit.

Joshua 1: 8-9

This book of the law shall not depart out of thy mouth; but thou shalt meditate therein day and night, that thou mayest observe to do according to all that is written therein: for then thou shalt make thy way prosperous, and then thou shalt have good success.

Have not I commanded thee? Be strong and of a good courage; be not afraid, neither be thou dismayed: for the LORD thy God is with thee whithersoever thou goest.

Proverbs 8: 12-21

I wisdom dwell with prudence, and find out knowledge of witty inventions.

The fear of the LORD is to hate evil: pride, and arrogancy, and the evil way, and the froward mouth, do I hate.

Counsel is mine, and sound wisdom: I am understanding; I have strength.

By me kings reign, and princes decree justice.

By me princes rule, and nobles, even all the judges of the earth.

I love them that love me; and those that seek me early shall find me.

Riches and honour are with me; yea, durable riches and righteousness.

My fruit is better than gold, yea, than fine gold; and my revenue than choice silver.

I lead in the way of righteousness, in the midst of the paths of judgment:

That I may cause those that love me to inherit substance; and I will fill their treasures.

CHAPTER XVIII

GOD GIVES US BOLDNESS, LOVE, AND WISDOM

When you read the title of this chapter, did you say to yourself that I lack inspiration because I just spoke about wisdom and am now repeating it? I'm sorry to disappoint you, but it's hard for me to untie what God has decided to keep attached. By the way, he wanted to tell us that he puts a spirit of confidence in us, but he attached it to wisdom and love. I keep it that way because our God does his work perfectly well. I touched you in the previous chapter with this truth from God: Why are you afraid when I put confidence in you? Why do you feel weak when I put strength in you? And, moreover, I accompany it with love for good works and wisdom so that you can discern your rights from your non-rights. The Lord opened my eyes to a truth that has been very powerful for my life: Who are you according to God's data sheet? This question reminded me of a judge in Israel named Gideon. Israel was attacked from all sides by enemy countries, from which Midian and Gideon hid like everyone else and complained like everyone else without knowing that he was the one who had to deliver Israel from this powerful enemy. But do you know what God sees when reading your technical sheet? If not, have you ever wondered this?

Christ gives us peace and tells us not to be troubled (John 14:1, 27).

God gives us the spirit of confidence, love, and wisdom so that we have no fear (2 Timothy 1:7).

Stop diminishing yourself by constantly repeating to yourself, *I am afraid*. Did you realize that by saying this, you are clearly and simply repeating, *I possess fear*? My question to me and to you now is how can we possess such a bad thing that God did not give us?

God is shocked to hear this word from our lips when He declares it to us very clearly and simply: "I have not given you the spirit of fear, but of wisdom, love, and confidence."

I still remember my arrival at this young assembly in Quebec. The pastor took several Sundays to teach about the need for boldness in our endeavors. Courage, courage, courage.

I began to pray to receive this courage, this boldness, and this strength to resume all my beautiful projects abandoned for lack of courage. I received many beautiful responses from God: The Holy Spirit allowed my conscience to remember two things:

- Everything has a beginning, and wisdom is the beginning of everything.
- Perfect love banishes fear.

Let's get to work on building our confidence; God has already given it to us.

BIBLICAL REFERENCES

2 Timothy 1: 7

For God hath not given us the spirit of fear; but of power, and of love, and of a sound mind.

Proverbs 4: 7

Wisdom is the principal thing; therefore get wisdom: and with all thy getting get understanding.

Romans 8: 14-17

For as many as are led by the Spirit of God, they are the sons of God.

For ye have not received the spirit of bondage again to fear; but ye have received the Spirit of adoption, whereby we cry, Abba, Father.

The Spirit itself beareth witness with our spirit, that we are the children of God:

And if children, then heirs; heirs of God, and joint-heirs with Christ; if so be that we suffer with him, that we may be also glorified together.

Proverbs 8: 12-22

I wisdom dwell with prudence, and find out knowledge of witty inventions.

The fear of the LORD is to hate evil: pride, and arrogancy, and the evil way, and the froward mouth, do I hate.

Counsel is mine, and sound wisdom: I am understanding; I have strength.

By me kings reign, and princes decree justice.

By me princes rule, and nobles, even all the judges of the earth.

I love them that love me; and those that seek me early shall find me.

Riches and honour are with me; yea, durable riches and righteousness.

My fruit is better than gold, yea, than fine gold; and my revenue than choice silver.

I lead in the way of righteousness, in the midst of the paths of judgment:

That I may cause those that love me to inherit substance; and I will fill their treasures.

The LORD possessed me in the beginning of his way, before his works of old.

James 1: 5-8

If any of you lack wisdom, let him ask of God, that giveth to all men liberally, and upbraideth not; and it shall be given him.

But let him ask in faith, nothing wavering. For he that wavereth is like a wave of the sea driven with the wind and tossed.

For let not that man think that he shall receive any thing of the Lord.

A double minded man is unstable in all his ways.

1 John 4: 17-18

Herein is our love made perfect, that we may have boldness in the day of judgment: because as he is, so are we in this world.

There is no fear in love; but perfect love casteth out fear: because fear hath torment. He that feareth is not made perfect in love.

CHAPTER XIX

GOD OFFERS US A LIFE OF ABUNDANCE

The title here mentions abundance, but what God wants for us is more than abundance. Indeed, I just made a mistake by saying, "He wants." He not only wants abundance; He gives us abundance and more. Oh! But frankly, Madam; frankly, Sir; frankly, young man; frankly, young lady, how can you ignore for so long something that you are looking for and that God is offering you? If this information shocks you, know that you are not the only one. I was also affected by this discovery.

David said, "The LORD is my shepherd; I will not want" (Psalm 23:1). You may be thinking about a lot of money right now, but it's so much more than money. You are thinking of a lot of riches right now, but it is much more than that. Tell me just one thing you need that God, in His Word, hasn't already given you (us).

God gives us life in abundance (John 10:10).

Know this: today, God has called us to live in abundance, to be successful in all our endeavors (Joshua 1:8–9), and to live above all the evils that trouble the earth and which are to come (Ephesians 1:20–24; 2:4–7). The question is will you continue to ignore it? Or will you cross over to God's side, do His will, and receive His riches for your life?

BIBLICAL REFERENCES

Psalms 23

The LORD is my shepherd; I shall not want.

He maketh me to lie down in green pastures: he leadeth me beside the still waters.

He restoreth my soul: he leadeth me in the paths of righteousness for his name's sake.

Yea, though I walk through the valley of the shadow of death, I will fear no evil: for thou art with me; thy rod and thy staff they comfort me.

Thou preparest a table before me in the presence of mine enemies: thou anointest my head with oil; **my cup runneth over**.

Surely **goodness and mercy shall follow me all the days of my life**: and I will dwell in the house of the LORD forever.

John 10: 10

The thief cometh not, but for to steal, and to kill, and to destroy: I am come that they might have life, and that they might have it more abundantly.

2 Corinthians 9: 8

And God is able to make all grace abound toward you; that ye, always having all sufficiency in all things, may abound to every good work.

Malachi 3: 10

Bring ye all the tithes into the storehouse, that there may be meat in mine house, and prove me now herewith, saith the LORD of hosts, if I will *not open you the windows of heaven*, and *pour you out a blessing*, that there shall not be room enough to receive it.

Exodus 23: 25

And ye shall serve the LORD your God, and he shall bless thy bread, and thy water; and I will take sickness away from the midst of thee.

Joshua 1: 8-9

This book of the law shall not depart out of thy mouth; but thou shalt meditate therein day and night, that thou mayest observe to do according to all that is written therein: for then thou shalt make thy way prosperous, and then thou shalt have good success.

Have not I commanded thee? Be strong and of a good courage; be not afraid, neither be thou dismayed: **for the LORD thy God is with thee whithersoever thou goest.**

Psalms 2: 7-11

I will declare the decree: the LORD hath said unto me, Thou art my Son; this day have I begotten thee.

Ask of me, and I shall give thee the heathen for thine inheritance, and the uttermost parts of the earth for thy possession.

Thou shalt break them with a rod of iron; thou shalt dash them in pieces like a potter's vessel.

Be wise now therefore, O ye kings: *be instructed*, ye judges of the earth.

Serve the LORD with fear, and rejoice with trembling.

Ephesians 1: 16-23

I cease not to give thanks for you, making mention of you in my prayers;

That the God of our Lord Jesus Christ, the Father of glory, may give unto you the spirit of wisdom and revelation in the knowledge of him:

The eyes of your understanding being enlightened; that ye may know what is the hope of his calling, and *what the riches of the glory of his inheritance in the saints,*

And what is the exceeding greatness of his power to usward who believe, according to the working of his mighty power,

Which he wrought in Christ, when he raised him from the dead, and set him at his own right hand in the heavenly places,

Far above all principality, and power, and might, and dominion, and every name that is named, not only in this world, but also in that which is to come:

And hath put all things under his feet, and gave him to be the head over all things to the church,

Which is his body, the fulness of him that filleth all in all.

Ephesians 2 : 4-7

But God, who is rich in mercy, for his great love wherewith he loved us,

Even when we were dead in sins, hath quickened us together with Christ, (by grace ye are saved ;)

And hath raised us up together, *and made us sit together in heavenly places in Christ Jesus:*

That in the ages to come he might shew the exceeding riches of his grace in his kindness toward us through Christ Jesus.

CHAPTER XX
GOD COMMANDS US TO GLORIFY HIM ALWAYS

Do you know that God is your Creator? Yes, the one who decided to make you this wonderful being that you are is God. I was shocked the first time I became aware of how my heart works: the atria, the ventricles, the purification of blood and its return to my body. The biggest deal for me is the fact that my heart works like a pump. My heart is a pump that works 24 hours a day, 7 days a week, for all the years of my life (I'm approaching fifty). I do not add gasoline to it, I do not maintain it, and I only enjoy the favor of God. Are you suffering from heart failure or any heart problem and doctors tell you there is nothing they can do for you? If so, I have good news. God not only designs us and creates us in an exceptional way, but he is also able to repair the damage caused in our lives, for by the stripes of Christ, we are healed (Isaiah 53:5). It is only favor, grace, blessings, and extraordinary abundance.

There is even more. I just told you that God commands us to glorify him. The shock I received recently was that even though we are commanded to glorify Him, we happen to be the main beneficiaries of that glory. The Word of God tells us, when you are troubled, pray; when you rejoice, glorify God (James 5:13); when you glorify God, you are filled with the Holy Spirit (Ephesians 5:18–20). God puts his Spirit in us for a very particular work: to give us everything necessary to accomplish the project for which he designed us (1 Corinthians 12:11; 2:10; Jeremiah 29:11). Whether you know it or not, whether you are aware of it or not, you are created to accomplish noble projects that will lead to making a difference in this life.

Do you know the story of Gideon (Judges 6)? He was a judge in Israel and lived in the country, which was oppressed by Midian and other allied countries. Gideon hid in the caves when all the people sought refuge in them. He was complaining with all the people about the miseries of the land when one day, the angel of the Lord appeared to him, saying, "Hey! Valiant hero, arise! Go and deliver Israel from the hand of the Midianites." Gideon's shock was great. I wonder if you wouldn't be similarly shocked if you heard God speak to you about the plan he has for you too.

Back on topic. God gives us the Holy Spirit as comforter, teacher, revealer of the mysteries of God, counselor, guide, etcetera (1 Corinthians 2:10; John 16:13). Moreover, the Holy Spirit is in us to produce joy, among other things. Listen carefully to this loop of blessings, my friends: you are joyful; glorify God by speaking with hymns and spiritual songs; and in doing so, you fill yourselves with the Holy Spirit who is in you to produce joy. This ordinance clearly shows us that God wants our joy, peace, and more at all times. With God, we only win.

BIBLICAL REFERENCES

Isaiah 53: 5

But he was wounded for our transgressions, he was bruised for our iniquities: the chastisement of our peace was upon him; and with his stripes we are healed.

James 5: 13

Is any among you afflicted? Let him pray. **Is any merry? Let him sing psalms.**

1 Thessalonians 5: 16-19

Rejoice evermore.

Pray without ceasing.

In everything give thanks: for this is the will of God in Christ Jesus concerning you.

Quench not the Spirit.

Ephesians 5: 18-20

And be not drunk with wine, wherein is excess; but be filled with the Spirit;

Speaking to yourselves in psalms and hymns and spiritual songs, singing and making melody in your heart to the Lord;

Giving thanks always for all things unto God and the Father in the name of our Lord Jesus Christ;

Galatians 5: 22-23

But the fruit of the Spirit is love, joy, peace, longsuffering, gentleness, goodness, faith,

Meekness, temperance: against such there is no law.

1 Corinthians 2: 10

But God hath revealed them unto us by his Spirit: for the Spirit searcheth all things, yea, the deep things of God.

1 Corinthians 12: 11

But all these worketh that one and the selfsame Spirit, dividing to every man severally as he will.

Jeremiah 29: 11-12

For I know the thoughts that I think toward you, saith the LORD, thoughts of peace, and not of evil, to give you an expected end.

Then shall ye call upon me, and ye shall go and pray unto me, and I will hearken unto you.

John 16: 13

Howbeit when he, the Spirit of truth, is come, he will guide you into all truth: for he shall not speak of himself; but whatsoever he shall hear, that shall he speak: and he will shew you things to come.

CHAPTER XXI
GOD PUTS HIS SPIRIT IN US

Man is tripartite; did you know that? The Word of God tells us that man is a spirit who dwells in a body (made of mud) and who has a soul (Genesis 2:7; Job 32:8). There is one thing in the Bible that I really like: the main reason for Jesus' coming to earth (Luke 4:18–21). He came to set the oppressed free, and his mission is accomplished. This is why I live according to the freedom God has placed for me in Christ. Hallelujah!

Are you a spirit or a body mass? Your answer to this simple and short question is of capital importance and even crucial; it defines your appreciation of yourself. The global system programs us into so many things: you have a beautiful mouth, you have a beautiful color, you have beautiful eyes. Who decided on the criteria of beauty? And yet we accept these things as if they were part of ourselves, to the point of hearing some people declare with their own mouth: I am ugly despite their strength, their health, their kindness, their faithfulness, their patience, etc. Is it so difficult to declare that I am a spirit because my God, who never lies, tells me so in his word?

We decide what we want for our lives. Many people think that it is impossible not to lie, steal, cheat, or simply sin. They are right. But God puts his Spirit within us to make our task easier. God himself tells us through his word that the flesh lusts contrary to those of the spirit, and the spirit lusts contrary to those of the flesh (Galatians 5:16–18). The two don't mix well. But when we accept the grace of God offered in Jesus Christ, it is no longer the flesh that decides for us; it is the Spirit of God in us. I told you earlier that the presence of the Spirit of God brings us love as well as these attributes: joy, peace, patience, kindness, faith/fidelity, gentleness, benevolence, and temperance. Imagine for a moment: God decides your words, your thoughts, your actions. It is no longer you who live in this body; it is God himself.

If you rely on your strength to get you out of sin, your failure is assured. But if you count on God to overcome all of life's obstacles, you are more than victorious.

We are more than conquerors. Hallelujah!

The Spirit of God in us is the key that opens all doors. It produces in us the love of God, the perfect love that banishes fear, and more. It is the seal that identifies us with God. It is the bond that attaches us to our Father. Our position in the realm of God is established by the measure of the Spirit dwelling within us.

BIBLICAL REFERENCES

Genesis 2: 7

And the LORD God formed man of the dust of the ground, and breathed into his nostrils the breath of life; and man became a living soul.

Job 32: 7-9

I said, Days should speak, and multitude of years should teach wisdom.

But there is a spirit in man: and the inspiration of the Almighty giveth them understanding.

Great men are not always wise: neither do the aged understand judgment.

Luke 4: 18-21

The Spirit of the Lord is upon me, because he hath anointed me to preach the gospel to the poor; he hath sent me to heal the brokenhearted, to preach deliverance to the captives, and recovering of sight to the blind, to set at liberty them that are bruised,

To preach the acceptable year of the Lord.

And he closed the book, and he gave it again to the minister, and sat down. And the eyes of all them that were in the synagogue were fastened on him.

And he began to say unto them, this day is this scripture fulfilled in your ears.

Galatians 5: 16-18, 22-23

This I say then, Walk in the Spirit, and ye shall not fulfil the lust of the flesh.

For the flesh lusteth against the Spirit, and the Spirit against the flesh: and these are contrary the one to the other: so that ye cannot do the things that ye would.

But if ye be led of the Spirit, ye are not under the law.

But the fruit of the Spirit is love, joy, peace, longsuffering, gentleness, goodness, faith,

Meekness, temperance: against such there is no law.

Ephesians 5: 18- 21

And be not drunk with wine, wherein is excess; but be filled with the Spirit;

Speaking to yourselves in psalms and hymns and spiritual songs, singing and making melody in your heart to the Lord;

Giving thanks always for all things unto God and the Father in the name of our Lord Jesus Christ;

Submitting yourselves one to another in the fear of God.

1 John 4: 13, 18-19

Hereby know we that we dwell in him, and he in us, because he hath given us of his Spirit.

There is no fear in love; but perfect love casteth out fear: because fear hath torment. He that feareth is not made perfect in love.

We love him, because he first loved us.

Romans 8: 9-11

But ye are not in the flesh, but in the Spirit, if so be that the Spirit of God dwell in you. *Now if any man have not the Spirit of Christ, he is none of his.*

And if Christ be in you, the body is dead because of sin; but the Spirit is life because of righteousness.

But if the Spirit of him that raised up Jesus from the dead dwell in you, he that raised up Christ from the dead shall also quicken your mortal bodies by his Spirit that dwelleth in you.

John 14: 16-17

And I will pray the Father, and he shall give you another Comforter, that he may abide with you for ever;

Even the Spirit of truth; whom the world cannot receive, because it seeth him not, neither knoweth him: but ye know him; for he dwelleth with you, and shall be in you.

Colossians 3: 14

And above all these things put on charity, which is the bond of perfectness.

Galatians 2: 20

I am crucified with Christ: nevertheless I live; yet not I, but Christ liveth in me: and the life which I now live in the flesh I live by the faith of the Son of God, who loved me, and gave himself for me.

Ephesians 1: 13-14

In whom ye also trusted, after that ye heard the word of truth, the gospel of your salvation: *in whom also after that ye believed, ye were sealed with that Holy Spirit of promise,*

Which is the earnest of our inheritance until the redemption of the purchased possession, unto the praise of his glory.

CHAPTER XXII

SONS AND DAUGHTERS OF GOD BY ADOPTION

Are you familiar with the adoption process, where a person or couple decides to pass off a child legally as their own? In this chapter, the adopting parent is not just any person or couple; it is God himself who adopted us in Christ (Ephesians 1:5). Hallelujah!

We have beautiful examples of adoption in the Bible: Moses was adopted by the pharaoh's daughter; Esther was adopted by her uncle Mordecai; Ruth was adopted by Naomi; and even our Lord Jesus was adopted by his earthly father, Joseph.

Many adopted children, at a certain stage in their lives, think that adoption is not a good thing. But I tell you, my friends, that it takes much more than a mother's love to adopt a child. As a biological mother of two children, I find that filial love is established by God. But the love of a person (a stranger, a neighbor, etc.) requires a love stronger than filial love. I want to take the time to salute all these strong people who took the initiative to adopt a child; you are true lovers. Well done!

The Bible tells us about the only Son of God: Jesus. He sacrificed him as a ransom so that, in him, we could also become his sons. I see there a legitimate son who fights to the death so that foreign children are adopted by his parents. I only find that in Christ. Through him, we went from creatures to sons, from sinners to saints, from condemned to saved. It's extraordinary.

It just takes a little word to understand this mystery: faith.

Knowing that God is the truth, that he is confused with his word, and that his word tells us that he adopts us as his own sons and daughters in Christ Jesus (John 1:12-13), our duty is to believe. Science tells us that the earth revolves around the sun. Do you believe it or not? We all believe it.

So, take this small act of faith and declare these words:

God, thank you for offering me adoption through your son, Jesus Christ.

I know that you are the truth and that your word is the truth.

I receive your offer at this moment, and by this declaration of faith,

I receive the power to become your child, according to your word.

In the name of my Lord and Savior Jesus, who died, was buried, rose again, was received into heaven, and sits at your right hand, Amen!

We all agree that adoption is a common thing. However, while a biological child carries the genetic traits of their parents, this is not the case for adopted children, and God, our Father, knows this well. To compensate for this lack, he comes to remain in us through his Spirit, so that we can carry his genetic traits. Let's analyze this together: God is love (1 John 4:7-8), and He puts His Spirit in us with the mission of producing in us the fruit of the spirit: love (Galatians 5:22). Thus, by letting ourselves be guided by the Spirit of God and filling ourselves with his presence, we will manifest the nature of our heavenly Father, which is love.

BIBLICAL REFERENCES

Ephesians 1: 3-14

Blessed be the God and Father of our Lord Jesus Christ, who hath blessed us with all spiritual blessings in heavenly places in Christ:

According as he hath chosen us in him before the foundation of the world, that we should be holy and without blame before him in love:

Having predestinated us unto the adoption of children by Jesus Christ to himself, according to the good pleasure of his will,

To the praise of the glory of his grace, wherein he hath made us accepted in the beloved.

In whom we have redemption through his blood, the forgiveness of sins, according to the riches of his grace;

Wherein he hath abounded toward us in all wisdom and prudence;

Having made known unto us the mystery of his will, according to his good pleasure which he hath purposed in himself:

That in the dispensation of the fullness of times he might gather together in one all things in Christ, both which are in heaven, and which are on earth; even in him:

In whom also we have obtained an inheritance, being predestinated according to the purpose of him who worketh all things after the counsel of his own will:

That we should be to the praise of his glory, who first trusted in Christ.

In whom ye also trusted, after that ye heard the word of truth, the gospel of your salvation: in whom also after that ye believed, ye were sealed with that Holy Spirit of promise, Which is the earnest of our inheritance until the redemption of the purchased possession, unto the praise of his glory.

Romans 8: 14-17

For as many as are led by the Spirit of God, they are the sons of God.

For ye have not received the spirit of bondage again to fear; but *ye have received the Spirit of adoption*, whereby we cry, Abba, Father.

The Spirit itself beareth witness with our spirit, that we are the children of God:

And if children, then heirs; heirs of God, and joint-heirs with Christ; if so be that we suffer with him, that we may be also glorified together.

John 1: 12-13

But as many as received him, to them gave he p*ower to become the sons of God*, even to them that believe on his name:

Which were born, not of blood, nor of the will of the flesh, nor of the will of man, but of God.

1 John 4: 7-8

Beloved, let us love one another: for love is of God; and every one that loveth is born of God, and knoweth God.

He that loveth not knoweth not God; for *God is love*.

Galatians 5: 22-23

But **the fruit of the Spirit is love**, joy, peace, longsuffering, gentleness, goodness, faith,

Meekness, temperance: against such there is no law.

John 1: 1-3

In the beginning was the Word, and the Word was with God, and *the Word was God*.

The same was in the beginning with God.

All things were made by him; and without him was not anything made that was made.

CHAPTER XXIII
GOD IS SOVEREIGN – LET US GLORIFY HIM!

I consider myself to God as my car or my house is to me. The difference is that I am an intelligent woman—gifted with thought, filled with wisdom, and endowed with the capacity to love my Creator and to be indebted to him. A car is easier to understand. But I pay for my car or my house, so they are mine, and I can do what I want with them. Do you know that God is not accountable to anyone for creation? He created the universe by his wisdom and according to his will alone (Genesis 1). Our God is sovereign. He does what he wants, when he wants, where he wants, for whom he wants, and how he wants. Do you think he's asking for too much?

I told you previously about an ordinance from God: He commands us to give Him glory. We all agree that this is an order. However, in doing it, we fill ourselves with His Spirit, who fills us with all the attributes of God as well as the abilities we need to accomplish God's purposes in our lives (Jeremiah 29:11).

Let us think of the immensity of his works, the greatness of his love, and his great projects of hope and peace for our lives, then answer this question: Why not just respond to his requests? Let us give glory to God. He is the only one who deserves the glory.

BIBLICAL REFERENCES

Genesis 1: 3, 6, 9, 14, 20, 24, 26

And God said, Let there be light: and there was light. And God said, Let there be a firmament in the midst of the waters, and let it divide the waters from the waters.

And God said, Let the waters under the heaven be gathered together unto one place, and let the dry land appear: and it was so.

And God said, Let there be lights in the firmament of the heaven to divide the day from the night; and let them be for signs, and for seasons, and for days, and years:

And God said, Let the waters bring forth abundantly the moving creature that hath life, and fowl that may fly above the earth in the open firmament of heaven.

And God said, Let the earth bring forth the living creature after his kind, cattle, and creeping thing, and beast of the earth after his kind: and it was so.

And God said, Let us make man in our image, after our likeness: and let them have dominion over the fish of the sea, and over the fowl of the air, and over the cattle, and over all the earth, and over every creeping thing that creepeth upon the earth.

1 Timothy 6: 13-15

I give thee charge in the sight of God, who quickeneth all things, and before Christ Jesus, who before Pontius Pilate witnessed a good confession;

That thou keep this commandment without spot, unrebukable, until the appearing of our Lord Jesus Christ:

Which in his times he shall shew, who is the blessed and only Potentate, the King of kings, and Lord of lords;

Psalms 150

Praise ye the LORD. Praise God in his sanctuary: praise him in the firmament of his power.

Praise him for his mighty acts: praise him according to his excellent greatness.

Praise him with the sound of the trumpet: praise him with the psaltery and harp.

Praise him with the timbrel and dance: praise him with stringed instruments and organs.

Praise him upon the loud cymbals: praise him upon the high sounding cymbals.

Let everything that hath breath praise the LORD. Praise ye the LORD.

Psalms 96: 1-3

O sing unto the LORD a new song: sing unto the LORD, all the earth.

Sing unto the LORD, bless his name; shew forth his salvation from day to day.

Declare his glory among the heathen, his wonders among all people.

Psalms 50: 14

Offer unto God thanksgiving; and pay thy vows unto the most High.

1 Chronicles 16: 25-29

For great is the LORD, and greatly to be praised: he also is to be feared above all gods.

For all the gods of the people are idols: but the LORD made the heavens.

Glory and honour are in his presence; strength and gladness are in his place.

Give unto the LORD, ye kindreds of the people, give unto the LORD glory and strength.

Give unto the LORD the glory due unto his name: bring an offering, and come before him: worship the LORD in the beauty of holiness.

Psalms 135: 6

Whatsoever the LORD pleased, that did he in heaven, and in earth, in the seas, and all deep places.

Job 33: 1-15

Wherefore, Job, I pray thee, hear my speeches, and hearken to all my words.

Behold, now I have opened my mouth, my tongue hath spoken in my mouth.

My words shall be of the uprightness of my heart: and my lips shall utter knowledge clearly.

The spirit of God hath made me, and the breath of the Almighty hath given me life.

If thou canst answer me, set thy words in order before me, stand up.

Behold, I am according to thy wish in God's stead: I also am formed out of the clay.

Behold, my terror shall not make thee afraid, neither shall my hand be heavy upon thee.

Surely thou hast spoken in mine hearing, and I have heard the voice of thy words, saying,

I am clean without transgression, I am innocent; neither is there iniquity in me.

Behold, he findeth occasions against me, he counteth me for his enemy,

He putteth my feet in the stocks, he marketh all my paths.

Behold, in this thou art not just: I will answer thee, that *God is greater than man*.

Why dost thou strive against him? *For he giveth not account of any of his matters.*

For God speaketh once, yea twice, yet man perceiveth it not.

In a dream, in a vision of the night, when deep sleep falleth upon men, in slumberings upon the bed;

Psalms 115: 3

But our God is in the heavens: he hath done whatsoever he hath pleased.

Isaiah 46: 10

Declaring the end from the beginning, and from ancient times the things that are not yet done, saying, My counsel shall stand, and I will do all my pleasure:

Daniel 4: 35

And all the inhabitants of the earth are reputed as nothing: and he doeth according to his will in the army of heaven, and among the inhabitants of the earth: and none can stay his hand, or say unto him, What doest thou?

2 Chronicles 20: 6

And said, O LORD God of our fathers, art not thou God in heaven? and rulest not thou over all the kingdoms of the heathen? and in thine hand is there not power and might, so that none is able to withstand thee?

Psalms 47: 2

For the LORD most high is terrible; he is a great King over all the earth.

Acts 5: 34-39

Then stood there up one in the council, a Pharisee, named Gamaliel, a doctor of the law, had in reputation among all the people, and commanded to put the apostles forth a little space;

And said unto them, Ye men of Israel, take heed to yourselves what ye intend to do as touching these men.

For before these days rose up Theudas, boasting himself to be somebody; to whom a number of men, about four hundred, joined themselves: who was slain; and all, as many as obeyed him, were scattered, and brought to nought.

After this man rose up Judas of Galilee in the days of the taxing, and drew away much people after him: he also perished; and all, even as many as obeyed him, were dispersed.

And now I say unto you, Refrain from these men, and let them alone: for if this counselor this work be of men, it will come to nought:

But *if it be of God, ye cannot overthrow it; lest haply ye be found even to fight against God.*

CHAPTER XXIV
GOD WANTS US TO BE GOOD AND KIND

In walking with God, I have learned that there is a difference between being sensitive and being humble. I was shocked by this revelation when the Holy Spirit told me, "Sensitivity is of the devil." Did you know? Are you also shocked to hear it, like I was?

When I receive a revelation, my first reaction is to pray for the Word of God that confirms the revelation. God does not lie, nor will he ever lie; he will always act in accordance with his word (Numbers 23:19). I do the same thing when I hear a message from a man or woman of God, even if he speaks in the name of the Lord. This is how I manage to differentiate between what God wants for my life and what religion dictates to me. I thank the Lord for that.

God asks us to be good, to endure, to love, and to help those in need, but he does not ask us to let ourselves be abused by others or to live like helpless victims. Sensitivity is not even mentioned in the exhortation texts. I don't know how many times I have heard or how many examples I could have given to show you how bad people take advantage of the sensitivity of good people in order to do them harm. Isaiah the prophet prophesied that the Lord Jesus would be filled with the Spirit of wisdom and understanding, the Spirit of counsel and might, the Spirit of knowledge, and the fear of the Lord (Isaiah 11:2–5). God puts His Spirit within us to produce love and its attributes, including kindness (Galatians 5:22–23). God tells us to love our enemies because in doing so, we heap burning coals on their heads (Proverbs 25:21–22), and he tells us: I am the God of vengeance. I really like this God. He is the God of vengeance (Romans 12:19).

Dear reader, your kindness and benevolence must be accompanied by wisdom at all times. Listen to the word of God, which tells us to bear with widows and which specifies "those who are truly widows," that is to say... and a description is made of what wisdom defines as a widow (1 Timothy 5:3, 5, 9–10). The word of God invites us to give, but it tells us to give without constraint, to lend as if we do not expect repayment (Luke 6:35), but if the loan will cause any problems in the future, don't do it. I could give you many illustrations of the word of God, which deals with goodness; they are all done with moderation. Let us use wisdom at all times.

When God asks us to be good, this does not mean that he hands us over as eternal victims. On the contrary, he knows that we do not have to defend ourselves because he is our defender, our protector, and our provider, and above all, he is the one who avenges on our behalf. Alleluia!

BIBLICAL REFERENCES

Numbers 23: 19

God is not a man that he should lie; neither the son of man that he should repent: hath he said, and shall he not do it? Or hath he spoken, and shall he not make it good?

Isaiah 11: 2-5

And the spirit of the LORD shall rest upon him, the spirit of wisdom and understanding, the spirit of counsel and might, the spirit of knowledge and of the fear of the LORD;

And shall make him of quick understanding in the fear of the LORD: and he shall not judge after the sight of his eyes, neither reprove after the hearing of his ears:

But with righteousness shall he judge the poor, and reprove with equity for the meek of the earth: and he shall smite the earth: with the rod of his mouth, and with the breath of his lips shall he slay the wicked.

And righteousness shall be the girdle of his loins, and faithfulness the girdle of his reins.

Galatians 5: 22-23

But the fruit of the Spirit is love, joy, peace, longsuffering, gentleness, goodness, faith,

Meekness, temperance: against such there is no law.

Proverbs 25: 21-22

If thine enemy be hungry, give him bread to eat; and if he be thirsty, give him water to drink:

For thou shalt heap coals of fire upon his head, and the LORD shall reward thee.

Romans 12: 19

Dearly beloved, avenge not yourselves, but rather give place unto wrath: for it is written, Vengeance is mine; I will repay, saith the Lord.

1 Timothy 6: 1-2

Let as many servants as are under the yoke count their own masters worthy of all honour, that the name of God and his doctrine be not blasphemed.

And they that have believing masters, let them not despise them, because they are brethren; but rather do them service, because they are faithful and beloved, partakers of the benefit. These things teach and exhort.

Psalms 94: 1-2, 20-23

O Lord God, to whom vengeance belongeth; O God, to whom vengeance belongeth, shew thyself.

Lift up thyself, thou judge of the earth: render a reward to the proud.

Shall the throne of iniquity have fellowship with thee, which frameth mischief by a law?

They gather themselves together against the soul of the righteous, and condemn the innocent blood.

But the LORD is my defence; and my God is the rock of my refuge.

And he shall bring upon them their own iniquity, and shall cut them off in their own wickedness; yea, the LORD our God shall cut them off.

John 13: 34-35

A new commandment I give unto you, that ye love one another; as I have loved you, that ye also love one another.

By this shall all men know that ye are my disciples, if ye have love one to another?

Ephesians 4: 32

And be ye kind one to another, tenderhearted, forgiving one another, even as God for Christ's sake hath.

Colossians 3: 12-17

Put on therefore, as the elect of God, holy and beloved, bowels of mercies, kindness, humbleness of mind, meekness, longsuffering;

Forbearing one another, and forgiving one another, if any man have a quarrel against any: even as Christ forgave you, so also do ye.

And above all these things put on charity, which is the bond of perfectness.

And let the peace of God rule in your hearts, to which also ye are called in one body; and be ye thankful.

Let the word of Christ dwell in you richly in all wisdom; teaching and admonishing one another in psalms and hymns and spiritual songs, singing with grace in your hearts to the Lord.

And whatsoever ye do in word or deed, do all in the name of the Lord Jesus, giving thanks to God and the Father by him.

1 Timothy 5: 3, 5, 9-10

Honour widows that are widows indeed.

Now she that is a widow indeed, and desolate, trusteth in God, and continueth in supplications and prayers night and day.

Let not a widow be taken into the number under threescore years old, having been the wife of one man.

Well reported of for good works; if she have brought up children, if she have lodged strangers, if she have washed the saints' feet, if she have relieved the afflicted, if she have diligently followed every good work.

1 Samuel 2: 10

The adversaries of the LORD shall be broken to pieces; out of heaven shall he thunder upon them: the LORD shall judge the ends of the earth; and he shall give strength unto his king, and exalt the horn of his anointed.

CHAPTER XXV

HE IS THE GOD OF THE IMPOSSIBLE

It's no secret if I tell you that God and his actions are difficult to understand. This is also why it is said in his Word that the only way to serve God is to have faith. Faith is the only necessary and adequate material to serve and understand God. Salvation is a mystery. Grace is a mystery. The place of Christ is a mystery. Miracles are mysteries. Believers are a mystery to unbelievers. They even find us senseless. But we who are believers, through our faith in Jesus Christ, know in whom we believe. Hallelujah!

Have you ever found yourself in a situation where everyone tells you this case is impossible? An incurable illness, your salvation, your own person, an irrecoverable good? I am here to tell you that there is always a last resort at the end of these irrecoverable situations: the God of the Impossible. He's just waiting for us. I read in The Word of God the story of a man who had a child with an incurable illness. This nasty disease was intermittent (I remove it from your life here and now, in the name of Jesus), and each time it occurs, it throws the child into fire and/or water (Matthew 17:14). Remember that the wicked, the thief, comes only to steal, kill, and destroy (John 10:10). The child's father was desperate, but the last safe resort was there at the end of his situation, and he received his solution.

I think of this woman of prayer who relied heavily on this last resort as her only recourse. Her name is Mary, and she is a great blessing in my life. Her husband, initially a man of God, changed a lot at some point in their lives. He began flirting with younger women and despised his wife to the point of abandoning her in the house with their two children without warning. He rented a fully furnished apartment to live alone. But this woman of God, who counted on God as a last resort, I repeat, but as her only recourse in small and large situations like this, she brought the situation before God. She told me that I was not afraid of divorce or separation, but I was afraid of the impact it could have on the community of God. I was touched by his reflection, and I think that God was also touched by her commitment. The man was so well known for his devotion to God that no one could approach him about his attitude. It was shocking. God gave Mary the mission to fight her husband's spiritual battle, and she eventually brought him home. My spiritual father preached a message called "Supernatural Realities," where he spoke about the fourth dimension, the spiritual space where the life of a son and daughter of God is attackable by demons. I understood that you cannot serve God half-heartedly; it is a lifestyle in which you must continually perform. You may be one of those who have criticism or contempt for men of God. Know this: the lack of a revelation can make a big difference in a man's life. The word of God tells us: My people are destroyed because they lack knowledge (Hosea 4:6). I want to take the time to write you some important information: In Christ, God has made us a kingdom of priests. This means to me that if you choose to serve God, you must allow yourself to be open to God to hear the revelations He has for your life. God always speaks, and His channels of communication are everywhere (Job 33:14–18). Pray for your own connection, remembering that God often uses these people around you as a means of communication.

What you decide to believe matters a lot to who you are. I believe that God is the God of impossible situations, and therefore, economic, medical, family, and other news are only alarm bells for me to seek more in my heavenly inheritance. Your choice is truly yours.

BIBLICAL REFERENCES

John 10: 10

The thief cometh not, but for to steal, and to kill, and to destroy: I am come that they might have life, and that they might have it more abundantly.

Matthew 17: 14-21

And when they were come to the multitude, *there came to him a certain man, kneeling down to him, and saying,*

Lord, have mercy on my son: for he is lunatick, and sore vexed: for of times he falleth into the fire, and oft into the water.

And I brought him to thy disciples, and they could not cure him.

Then Jesus answered and said, O faithless and perverse generation, how long shall I be with you? How long shall I suffer you? Bring him hither to me.

And Jesus rebuked the devil; and he departed out of him: and *the child was cured from that very hour.*

Then came the disciples to Jesus apart, and said, Why could not we cast him out?

And Jesus said unto them, Because of your unbelief: for verily I say unto you, If ye have faith as a grain of mustard seed, ye shall say unto this mountain, Remove hence to yonder place; and it shall remove; and nothing shall be impossible unto you.

Howbeit this kind goeth not out but by prayer and fasting.

Hosea 4: 6

My people are destroyed for lack of knowledge: because thou hast rejected knowledge, I will also reject thee, that thou shalt be no priest to me: seeing thou hast forgotten the law of thy God, I will also forget thy children.

Job 33: 14- 18

For God speaketh once, yea twice, yet man perceiveth it not.

In a dream, in a vision of the night, when deep sleep falleth upon men, in slumberings upon the bed;

Then he openeth the ears of men, and sealeth their instruction,

¹⁷ That he may withdraw man from his purpose, and hide pride from man.

He keepeth back his soul from the pit, and his life from perishing by the sword.

Luke 1: 30-37

And the angel said unto her, Fear not, Mary: for thou hast found favour with God.

And, behold, thou shalt conceive in thy womb, and bring forth a son, and shalt call his name JESUS.

He shall be great, and shall be called the Son of the Highest: and the Lord God shall give unto him the throne of his father David:

And he shall reign over the house of Jacob forever; and of his kingdom there shall be no end.

Then said Mary unto the angel, how shall this be, seeing I know not a man?

And the angel answered and said unto her, The Holy Ghost shall come upon thee, and the power of the Highest shall overshadow thee: therefore also that holy thing which shall be born of thee shall be called the Son of God.

And, behold, thy cousin Elisabeth, she hath also conceived a son in her old age: and this is the sixth month with her, who was called barren.

For with God nothing shall be impossible.

Luke 18: 24-28

And when Jesus saw that he was very sorrowful, he said, how hardly shall they that have riches enter into the kingdom of God!

²⁵ For it is easier for a camel to go through a needle's eye, than for a rich man to enter into the kingdom of God.

And they that heard it said, who then can be saved?

And he said, *the things which are impossible with men are possible with God*.

Then Peter said, lo, we have left all, and followed thee.

Jeremiah 32: 26-27

Then came the word of the LORD unto Jeremiah, saying, Behold, I am the LORD, the God of all flesh: is there anything too hard for me?

FINAL WORDS

I arrived in Quebec in 2020, in the midst of the expansion of the famous COVID-19 pandemic. Two things quickly caught my attention: the customer service and the well-organized transportation system. I like it when it works well. This must flow from my understanding of God's will for us. I was in Montreal, and when I started to meet people, a third thing came to mind: everyone smiled at everyone—an extraordinary kindness. What a beautiful community, my God!

But when I began to learn about my new reality, my new environment, I was doubly shocked: on the one hand, by the visible place that the church occupies in Quebec society; on the other, by the apostasy within the vast majority of society.

- Oh yes! But I don't understand that!

Many Quebecers have been victims of certain acts of some leaders of the church, and as they stand up against the church, they also stand up against God. At least, that's my understanding of the matter.

- But no, beautiful, kind people with big hearts! You cannot confuse God and religion.

Certainly, religion is supposed to be an instrument to make God known, but I don't know how many times I drive at 90 km/h on a road where the maximum speed of 90 km/h is posted and other cars pass me with a speed of 100, 110,

125, or even more, whatever. The posted speed is there, but drivers do their own thing. It cannot be the fault of the government authority that carries out road checks, the one that takes care of transport, or, quite simply, the government.

This book is intended to be a wake-up call to tell the world, "DO NOT CONFUSE GOD WITH RELIGION." God is not religion. You may then be wondering, *what is religion for*? Or what's the point of going to church?

I could just testify how good it is to be able to share God's love with brothers and sisters, to be among brothers and sisters and be able to offer unparalleled adoration to our ALL-POWERFUL God. I am going to return again to the word of God to present this to you:

Psalms 133

Behold, oh! How pleasant it is, how sweet it is for brothers to dwell together! It is like the precious oil which, poured on the head, descends on the beard, on the beard of Aaron, which descends on the hem of his garments. It is like the dew of Hermon, which descends on the mountains of Zion; For there the Lord sends blessing, Life, for eternity.

I like this saying, which says, we are not going to reinvent the wheel. It is not worth the trouble.

God wants perfect unity between us. God himself said of the men preparing to build the Tower of Babel: "They are united - No one will be able to stop their project."

Christ prayed that we would be united.

John 17: 20-21

Neither pray I for these alone, but for them also which shall believe on me through their word; That they all may be one; as thou, Father, art in me, and I in thee, that they also may be one in us: that the world may believe that thou hast sent me. God does not want division in his kingdom. He wants us to be united.

God does not want division in his kingdom. He wants us to be united.

Matthew 18: 19-20

Again I say unto you, That if two of you shall agree on earth as touching any thing that they shall ask, it shall be done for them of my Father which is in heaven. For where two or three are gathered together in my name, there am I in the midst of them.

Romans 16: 17-18

Now I beseech you, brethren, mark them which cause divisions and offences contrary to the doctrine which ye have learned; and avoid them. For they that are such serve not our Lord Jesus Christ, but their own belly; and by good words and fair speeches deceive the hearts of the simple.

Furthermore, induction into the Kingdom of God is done through the laying of hands by an elder. Let's read the story of Cornelius in the book of Acts, chapter 10.

Acts 10: 3-5, 19-20, 34-35, 44-48

He saw in a vision evidently about the ninth hour of the day an angel of God coming in to him, and saying unto him, Cornelius. And when he looked on him, he was afraid, and said, What is it, Lord? And he said unto him, Thy prayers and thine alms are come up for a memorial before God. And now send men to Joppa, and call for one Simon, whose surname is Peter: While Peter thought on the vision, the Spirit said unto him, Behold, three men seek thee. Arise therefore, and get thee down, and go with them, doubting nothing: for I have sent them. Then Peter opened his mouth, and said, Of a truth I perceive that God is no respecter of persons: But in every nation he that feareth him, and worketh righteousness, is accepted with him. While Peter yet spake these words, the Holy Ghost fell on all them which heard the word. And they of the circumcision which believed were astonished, as many as came with Peter, because that on the Gentiles also was poured out the gift of the Holy Ghost. For they heard them speak with tongues, and magnify God. Then answered Peter, Can any man forbid water, that these should not be baptized, which have received the Holy Ghost as well as we? And he commanded them to be baptized in the name of the Lord. Then prayed they him to tarry certain days.

I offer you through these writings a basis for the construction of this unity for which Christ himself prayed to the Father. This must be his only prayer to God that awaits an answer. So, if one believes that Mary is a virgin and the other does not, it doesn't matter. We ALL know that God is the Creator and that Jesus, our Lord, is the Savior of humanity.

One believes that Saturday is the consecrated day and the other Sunday; it does not matter; our salvation does not come from the day of consecration but from God, who is the master of times and circumstances.

Dear friends, the enemies of God are regrouping and unifying, and we must change our approach. Let us opt for unity as our Lord taught us.

Let us always remember that in a short time, we will be together with one heart, with one voice, with the Lord, to glorify our God forever. THAT'S THE POINT.

Let us build our unity on a solid foundation.

God is the only one who deserves all the glory. Doing His will is our reason for being. Meeting his expectations fulfills his desires. **The division has failed!**

Key Biblical Verses

John 3: 16-17

For God so loved the world, that he gave his only begotten Son, that whosoever believeth in him should not perish, but have everlasting life.

For God sent not his Son into the world to condemn the world; but that the world through him might be saved.

John 1: 12-13

But as many as received him, to them gave he power to *become the sons of God*, even to them that believe on his name:

Which were born, not of blood, nor of the will of the flesh, nor of the will of man, but of God.

Romans 8: 14-17

For as many as are led by the Spirit of God, they are the sons of God.

For ye have not received the spirit of bondage again to fear; but ye have received the Spirit of adoption, whereby we cry, Abba, Father.

The Spirit itself beareth witness with our spirit, that we are the children of God:

And if children, then heirs; heirs of God, and joint-heirs with Christ; if so be that we suffer with him, that we may be also glorified together.

AUTHOR'S NOTE

This book is aimed at believers and non-believers who wish to know or at least deepen their knowledge about the person of God and his will for us, men. Disputes between religions are not covered here because I believe we have the right to know the truth that truly matters according to God. I have seen the divisions, the distractions, the demands, the confusions, and the lies that trouble the world and even the people of God, which disharmonize the body of Christ and prevent the unity of the community for which our Lord prayed before his elevation to the heavenly places at the right hand of the Father. The ego took over. I have come to lay down my stone to rebuild the edifice of unity in the community of sons and daughters of the living and true God. May God, in his infinite grace, help you to grasp this significance and become part of this urgent response to Christ's prayer, long-awaited by God Himself.

Father, I pray that they may be ONE

As we are one.

Let it be so in the name of Jesus!

70 precious words worth 1,000,000

Acts 20: 28-30

"Take heed therefore unto yourselves, and to all the flock, over the which the Holy Ghost hath made you overseers, to feed the church of God, which he hath purchased with his own blood.

For I know this, that after my departing shall grievous wolves enter in among you, not sparing the flock.

Also of your own selves shall men arise, speaking perverse things, to draw away disciples after them."

"God Without Religion" is a unique book that presents you with an innovative vision of the quest for God while freeing you from the traditional constraints of religion. Wisdom is the key, and God gives it simply by asking.

The main messages of this book are:

1. God is not religion, and
2. The essence of God's will for humanity meets the useful totality of man's needs.

However, God is and will remain a mystery. Therefore, this book only introduces the person of God; the Holy Spirit is the boss when it comes to teaching who God is and what His will is.

One thing is certain: this work is the author's contribution in the process of understanding who God really is.

If you enjoyed the book, please leave a review on Amazon.

www.ingramcontent.com/pod-product-compliance
Lightning Source LLC
Chambersburg PA
CBHW011522070526
44585CB00022B/2499